Diagnosis and Beyond

Counselling psychology contributions
to understanding human distress

Editor

Martin Milton

PCCS Books
Ross-on-Wye

First published 2012

PCCS BOOKS Ltd
2 Cropper Row
Alton Road
Ross-on-Wye
Herefordshire
HR9 5LA
UK
Tel +44 (0)1989 763900
www.pccs-books.co.uk

**Diagnosis and Beyond: Counselling psychology contributions
to understanding human distress**

A CIP catalogue record for this book is available from the British Library

ISBN 978 1 906254 37 7

Cover image and all images throughout © Martin Milton
Cover design by Old Dog Graphics
Printed by ImprintDigital, Exeter, UK

Contents

Dedication

To Stuart who lets me think and Jordan who stops me.

Acknowledgements

Thank you to everyone who influenced this book, whether it be clients, research participants, teachers, therapists or supervisors in the field or friends and family in our personal lives. Your contribution to our thinking is very much appreciated.

Special acknowledgement must be made to the clients who the contributors have had the honour of working with throughout their careers. It is your courage and perseverance that has taught us so much about what lies beyond diagnosis and the importance of realising that diagnosis may only be the first step on the road to a good life. We hope you understand that the decision to use anonymised and composite examples rather than specific stories was made out of respect, rather than wanting to change your experience. Where your specific story was used, we thank you for your permission to do so. Either way we think that the book is enormously enriched by your contribution.

Martin Milton would like to thank all of the contributors – the brief was not easy and it has been wonderful to work with such enthusiastic and creative people.

Roly Fletcher: I am indebted to Dr Amanda Redvers for her assistance with this chapter, including the generation and debate of ideas and her help in expressing these.

Lucy Atcheson: I would like to thank everyone I have ever clinically worked with for enriching my knowledge of anxiety.

Tim Knowlson: I would like to thank Martin Milton for his support and giving me this opportunity. I would also like to thank Jamie Robinson for listening to me talk about this chapter for a long time.

Foreword

Professor Arlene Vetere

What a refreshing book! I share the vision of the contributors, put forward with compassion, that therapeutic practice needs to be grounded in clear, theory-based formulation, if we are to go beyond description and diagnosis and explore our full potential. Along with this, I found the authors to be emotionally present in their writing, in ways that captured and illuminated the significance of therapy as a secure base. In these ways they show how understanding can be expanded in a safe context, where people can begin to take emotional risks and reach out to others, rebuilding trust, a sense of security and hope for the future.

All the authors acknowledge the current debates and conflicts around the usefulness (or otherwise) of psychiatric diagnosis, but appear more concerned about the dominance of a medicalised approach to human distress and relationship dilemmas. They explore the limitations of a 'symptom'-based approach to understanding that marginalises consideration of people's competencies, strengths, resources, social support and resilience. The British Psychological Society (BPS), in its response to the American Psychiatric Association's *DSM-5* development, articulates a concern that

> clients and the general public are negatively affected by the continued and continuous medicalisation of their natural and normal responses to their experiences; responses which undoubtedly have distressing consequences which demand helping responses, but which do not reflect illness so much as normal individual variation. (BPS, 2011: 1)

One of my enduring concerns, and so well articulated in this book, is the absence of a theory base to the *DSM/ICD* classification systems. It is not only that there are problems with reliability, validity, co-morbidity and prognostic value, but that one possible organising substrate for many of these problems with affect regulation, safety and attachment (this is more than a reframing of 'symptoms') in early and current developmental and relational trauma, is neglected. The earlier insistence within the development of the *DSM* that it should be theory-free has come to haunt us. However, much of the therapeutic work described in the pages of this book emphasises the importance of (a) identifying and regulating emotions; (b) developing a wider repertoire of coping responses, to include soothing and calming; (c) increasing capacity for empathy; and (d) clearer, more straightforward communication of needs and wishes in our close relationships, in the development of psychological and interpersonal resilience. Such work is rooted in theoretical integration.

Following on from this, a further concern arises when we consider the medicalised diagnostic approach to therapy to be found in the UK National Institute for Health and Clinical Excellence (NICE) guidance (see website for range of guidance documents). The NICE approach emphasises evidence for therapy outcomes, and privileges types of evidence, with randomised controlled trials (RCTs) seen as superior, using such evidence to make recommendations for therapeutic practice. The NICE approach ignores the scientific literature on the significance of the therapeutic alliance in promoting change. Thus the NICE guidance could be read to assume that any therapist can work with the recommended approach for the diagnosed symptom or syndrome, without recourse to issues of 'fit', i.e. why any particular therapist is attracted to any particular theories of therapy and ways of working. In addition, there is some evidence that the commitment of the therapist to their chosen approach makes a contribution to the effectiveness of the work. This raises the ethical question of how we look after and support our therapists in the emotionally demanding and complex work that they do, and not least, whether distress and relationship dilemmas can be treated as if they are physical conditions.

The emphasis within NICE is outcomes, and yet many therapists' questions and concerns are also with process. Similarly we can think of process moments, or significant events in therapy, as small outcomes in their own right. In this way of thinking, therapists are curious about mediators of change, and even more importantly, mechanisms of change – going beyond 'how does it work?', to 'in what ways does it work?' If I refer back to the work of Sackett et al. (2000), who wrote in a context of identifying best practice in physical medicine, their emphasis was on the *integration* of clinical experience with the best available empirical evidence. Thus an exclusive focus on outcome evidence generated in RCTs gives rise to an expectation that therapy is a technology to be applied in a technocracy. It is of concern to me that this seems to be on the increase. RCTs often exclude 'statistical outliers' from the analysis, and yet this is what therapists need to know, i.e. what is happening for those people who appear to respond really very well, or not at all well. RCTs can make generalised statements that may not apply to every individual who seeks support with emotional and behavioural difficulties. Thus it is to be applauded that many of the therapeutic examples offered in this book are accounts of working at the extremes of emotional experience, where formulation is needed to pioneer understanding, and to encompass the complex interplay of history, experience, relationships and social discourses.

The authors do not play it safe, so to speak. They attempt to remove the blocks to happiness in people's lives, seeing happiness as incremental and achievable. They lead the way in challenging any exclusive reliance on diagnosis in therapeutic practice. I admire the elegance of their collective approach as they do not need to do this by any destructive means, such as diminishing the work of colleagues or the needs of people who wish to assume diagnostic practices or benefit from them. I take my hat off to them. I hope you enjoy reading this book as much as I did!

University of Surrey
January, 2012

References

British Psychological Society (2011). *Response to the American Psychiatric Association: DSM-5 Development.* Consultation Response Team, The British Psychological Society. Leicester: BPS.

Sackett, DL, Straus, SE, Richardson, WS, Rosenberg, W & Haynes, RB (2000). *Evidence-Based Medicine: How to practice and teach EBM* (2nd ed). New York: Churchill Livingstone.

Website

National Institute for Health and Clinical Excellence http://www.nice.org.uk/topic

Preface

Martin Milton

Diagnosis. We have probably all wanted it. We all resist it. All the time we feel healthy, clear and rationale we hate the idea of being 'labelled'. When suffering and uncertain we want to 'know'. 'Why am I like this? What is happening to me? Diagnose me Doc! Then cure me, make me feel better. When you have done that I can go back to my normal life, (my fantasy life?), where all is as I wish it could be.'

Diagnosis affects us all. Right now I can think of at least three diagnoses of physical pathology that I have. I have self-diagnosed the beginnings of a cold, I have haemochromotosis (and have had for many years) diagnosed by a gastroenterologist. I have been diagnosed with osteoarthritis in my hips by a surgeon. And that's just me, amongst those close to me we have diagnoses of coeliac disease, angina, psoriasis, rheumatoid arthritis, cancer … and the list goes on. And I know that we are not at all unusual in this respect. At times we have wanted these diagnoses as they have shed light on physical mysteries and offered clarity on whether there was a cure or simply ways to manage the condition. And where this has been possible we have experienced relief and a sense of purpose.

It is not just organic phenomena that humans diagnose; we also have a long history of subjecting emotional, psychological and sometimes cultural experiences to diagnosis too. This is both an implicit and explicit activity. Critics have identified ways in which there is an over-representation of specific groups in relation to some diagnoses, for example we see some studies showing that more women are diagnosed as 'having' borderline personality disorder than men; men are more likely to be diagnosed as having antisocial personality disorder (see Chapter 7). There is a large body of work that looks at the ways in which gender and sexual choices have led explicitly to diagnoses too. For example, sexual minorities have long been labelled with psychiatric diagnoses (see Milton et al., 2010; Coyle et al., 2001) and currently we see debate and controversy about diagnoses in the realm of gender identification (Tosh, 2011).

Within these debates competing claims are made. Diagnosis is seen as a way to facilitate health and well-being, whereas another perspective is that diagnosis is a way that people's emotional expression and behaviour is controlled (Foucault, 1989; Golsworthy, 2004; Milton et al., 2010).

Diagnosis and its human implications

Human distress, those experiences that we term 'anxiety', 'depression', 'OCD', 'psychosis' and the myriad of other difficulties that people bring to therapists, are often viewed as 'psychopathology'. When we see it this way, human distress is understood to be a thing (separate to the person) that affects people, a phenomenon that can be legitimately 'diagnosed', 'treated' and hopefully 'cured'. From within this perspective it is appropriate to 'medicalise' emotional experience. It is this view that has led to the establishment of the psychological and psychiatric professions; it is also this mindset that leads psychologists, psychiatrists and other therapists to develop 'evidence bases' for specific 'disorders' and manualised forms of 'treatment'.

This way of understanding psychological and emotional experiences links people to diagnostic frameworks such as the *Diagnostic and Statistical Manual of Mental Disorders (DSM-IV)* (American Psychiatric Association, 1994) and *International Statistical Classification of Diseases and Related Health Problems (ICD-10)* (World Health Organization, 1992), classification systems which are said to provide a 'shorthand' for describing issues faced by mental health services. As my colleagues and I have noted previously, this can make a great deal of sense, so much so that this has become a key perspective in many public sector health settings, in government policy and legal proceedings in the UK, US and elsewhere (Milton et al., 2010).

Regardless of the benefits or problems associated with diagnosis, it is important to remember that understandings of 'psychopathology' are negotiated and constructed via socio-cultural and historically specific meanings (Foucault, 1989; Golsworthy, 2004; Milton et al., 2010; Parker et al., 1995) and the medicalised view is but one – and it is not without its problems. In their work with clients, counselling psychologists recognise that there is an important aspect where therapy is fundamentally a meeting of two human beings, who come together to face up to and wrestle with some of the big issues affecting us all. Therapy, when therapeutic, is recognised as being collaborative and egalitarian, not imposed or 'delivered'. Therefore we have to go beyond diagnosis if we hope to understand and assist people in their struggle towards well-being.

For the purposes of this book, it is important to note that it is within this conflict and competition that counselling psychologists and other therapists find themselves. When working with clients we are continually navigating between grand narratives about psychological health and pathology on the one hand, and the attempt to find personalised accounts that are meaningful and helpful to individual clients. This is one of the tensions that my colleagues and I are exploring in this book. In various ways we touch on questions about the nature of diagnosis, the ways in which it can be experienced as helpful and can also be seen to be at the root of much personal misery. We look at the philosophical and the pragmatic issues, the social and the personal.

The book

While the authors of the different chapters engage with the concept of diagnostic categories to varying degrees, the key focus of the following accounts is to try to articulate ways of engaging with the tensions that exist. By engaging with the range of presenting problems and contexts as they do, the authors give a sense of how they work with clients in distress in creative and flexible ways. Readers will see how counselling psychology engages with, and also challenges, the medical model of professional–client relationships as it focuses on well-being rather than on understanding psychological difficulties as sickness and pathology.

Whether working in harmony with the prevailing view or challenging it, a key message from all of the contributors is that while it is possible to critique the concept of psychopathology and the use of classification systems, it is important not to deny the *reality* of the pain or suffering that clients bring to therapists. The contributors allow questions to be raised as to how they (and other relationally oriented therapists) can engage with clients and the difficulties they bring. The chapters explore different forms of distress, starting unapologetically from a point that sees human distress as a meaningful (albeit often terribly confusing and painful) experience. The contributors describe the wisdom that can be embedded within apparently meaningless experiences, and consider ways in which counselling psychologists and clients together can create understanding, hope and possibility through robust, relational therapeutic processes. The contributors go beyond diagnosis and describe the ways in which genuine human engagement and interaction offer enormous benefits to clients and those they are closest to. It is our hope that readers will accept the implicit invitation to do the same.

Dr Roly Fletcher sets the scene for us by contextualising the ways in which human distress has traditionally been conceptualised and therapeutic services have been structured. Roly reflects on the ways in which this impacts on clients and therapists alike and sheds light on how the 'system' can help – or hinder – individuals' attempts to grapple with the difficulties in their lives.

After the scene has been set, the contributors focus their attention on working with clients and specific forms of distress – what they mean and the ways that counselling psychologists engage with these clients.

In Chapters 2 and 3, Dr Joanna Jackson and Dr Lucy Atcheson look at some of the more prevalent forms of distress – 'depression' and 'anxiety' – that affect many millions of people today. Yet for all their familiarity, and perhaps partly because of it, the nature and meaning of these experiences often seem vague and elusive. In a very sensitive and personal reflection, Joanna explores the relational 'causes' of depression and considers the ways in which the relational dimension is important if recovery and growth are to be facilitated. Lucy considers anxiety and shows why it is more than some 'irrational' symptom but often a profound and meaningful aspect of people's lives that warrants time and attention to fully understand it. She also outlines the effect that anxiety can have on someone experiencing it.

In Chapter 4, Dr Lucy Atcheson and I explore a specific type of anxiety – phobia – and consider the ways in which phobias develop. As well as offering an insight into ways of working with phobias, Lucy and I try to go beyond the diagnosis and discuss the importance of changing the public understanding of phobias to one that recognises phobias as an everyday human emotion (albeit in extremis) rather than a pathological diagnosis.

Physical pain and the psychological distress associated with it are a core focus in Chapter 5. Dr Terry Boucher explores the questions of 'what is pain?' and 'how do we work with those with pain?' In doing so he explores issues of engagement and self-disclosure in relation to the relational aspects of the therapeutic process.

Chapter 6 is written by Dr Louise Brorstrom and looks at relational trauma. She shows how the understanding of trauma should not be limited to those actions that are well known to be traumatic – such phenomena as physical violence, sexual abuse and major losses. Louise looks at how mis-attunement, even when some might argue it is relatively small, can lead to trauma and can damage the person, especially when frequent and cumulative. Louise uses a case study to discuss the ways in which the interpersonal impact of trauma manifests in people's lives and in therapy.

In Chapter 7, Dr Tim Knowlson explores the experience of working with the issue of 'personality disorder'. In doing so he focuses on the experience of abandonment (real or feared) and how this frequently has a central role in this rather demonised and confusing experience. In particular, Tim offers us an insight into the way in which the issue of abandonment plays out in the therapeutic relationship, affecting both client and therapist in very powerful ways.

In the final chapter, the attention is turned to a wider issue, that of embodiment and Dr Ben Rumble explores the ways that the body often plays a significant role in psychological distress. Ben considers why therapy is enhanced when we think about and formulate the bodily dimension of psychological distress. He fleshes out this missing dimension by setting out a clinically salient model of embodiment which pays particular attention to the body as image and as sensation.

The reader

When preparing to read these contributions, the reader should note that no one approach to diagnosis or therapy is being advocated. We rejected the notion of another 'how to' book. So this is not a book that intends to show *the* way to understand an experience or a model-specific 'treatment' manual. It is a book about people's individual experiences which are quite unique – both as clients and as therapists. All contributors are alert to the limitations of the diagnostic project; there are differences in the degrees to which people engage in the medical model, in diagnostic activity, what they discuss with clients and so forth. You will also see a diverse range of styles – some that take a traditional psychological approach, others that engage in a much more philosophical style and others that push theory to the back and rely enormously on human-to-human engagement. In different sections of the book you will see explanations, descriptions of therapeutic dialogue and even a flow chart.

At this point all that is left to do is to invite the reader to move on to the rest of the book and to join us in exploring diagnosis and what is beyond. The contributors and I hope very much that you will approach this task as we did, curious but critical, considered but open to change and that this will allow you to find something to make you think, to debate, to discuss with colleagues and clients in your own efforts to work productively towards limiting misery and enhancing well-being.

References

American Psychiatric Association (1994). *Diagnostic and Statistical Manual of Mental Disorders* (4th ed). Washington, DC: American Psychiatric Association.

Coyle, A, Milton, M & Annesley, P (2001). The silencing of lesbian and gay voices in psycho – 'therapeutic' texts, training and practice. In MC Steffens & U Biechele (Eds) *Annual Review of Lesbian, Gay and Bisexual Issues in European Psychology, 1*, 95–124.

Foucault, M (1989). *Madness and Civilisation: A history of insanity in the age of reason.* London: Routledge.

Golsworthy, R (2004). Counselling psychology and psychiatric classification: Clash or co-existence? *Counselling Psychology Review, 19*(3), 23–9.

Milton, M, Craven, M & Coyle, A (2010). Understanding human distress: Moving beyond the concept of 'psychopathology'. In M Milton (Ed) *Therapy and Beyond: Counselling psychology contributions to therapeutic and social issues.* Chichester: Wiley Blackwell.

Parker, I, Georgaca, E et al (1995). *Deconstructing Pychopathology.* London: Sage.

Tosh, J (2011). Challenging queerphobic practice: Protesting Professor Ken Zucker's 'prevention' of gender diversity. *Psychology of Sexualities, 2*(1), 54–61.

World Health Organization (1992). *International Statistical Classification of Diseases and Related Health Problems* (10th rev). Geneva: World Health Organization.

1

Introduction:
Dealing with diagnoses

Roly Fletcher

Introduction

In the British National Health Service (NHS), psychiatric diagnosis is an integral part of a 'treatment pathway' for those referred for psychological therapy.[1] Whist I might not always agree with the diagnoses that are given, the majority of those I see for therapy have nevertheless received one long before they are referred to me. In fact, for many, receiving such a diagnosis (at least implicitly) is a requirement for them to be able to access services.

Given that a diagnosis alone can aid or bar people from accessing services it seems critical that practitioners[2] make themselves aware of what diagnosis is, why it is considered so vital, what exactly working with diagnosis might entail, and some of the potential pitfalls related to it. In this chapter I reflect upon these issues from a personal standpoint, particularly how diagnosis has helped or hindered my therapeutic work. Where appropriate I shall draw on my clinical experience to illustrate my thinking.[3]

---

1. Within mental health services, the people who use services often get referred to using a variety of terms, e.g. 'client', 'patient', 'people who use services', etc. Without wishing to enter into a debate about the implications of each of these, I shall use them interchangeably as seems appropriate.
2. I use the word 'practitioner' as I wish to address the multitude of professionals who work within such services including, but not exclusively, psychologists, psychoanalytic psychotherapists, psychiatrists, mental health nurses, social workers, counsellors and so on.
3. All clinical examples have been anonymised and disguised to protect the confidentiality of the client.

What is diagnosis? How does it link with the NHS?

The idea of diagnosis is historically linked with the medical model (at least in the language it uses), which suggests that 'health' difficulties are 'symptoms' of an 'illness' located within the 'patient'. It assumes that if the 'symptoms' can be properly categorised (diagnosed) this will lead to the application of a 'treatment' (pharmaceutical, surgical, medical, psychological or otherwise) to target the symptoms in predictable, measurable ways (Strawbridge & Woolfe, 2003). This way of viewing health extends beyond health practitioners, however, and is dominant within society as a whole. The government, for example, perpetuates this view through the tasking of the National Institute for Health and Clinical Excellence (NICE) to produce guidelines which claim to define the interventions that have the most positive impact on the 'symptoms' for each diagnosis. This way of thinking is then spread out to the public by the Department of Health which states 'You [the 'patient'] have the right to drugs and treatments that have been recommended by NICE for use in the NHS' (Department of Health, 2009: 6). The NHS is then monitored for its compliance with these guidelines by regulators such as the Care Quality Commision (CQC) who have the power to suspend or cancel a service if it fails to meet their standards of care (Care Quality Commision, 2010).

With such pressure applied, the NHS has little choice but to comply with the NICE guidelines and therefore adopt a diagnostic way of working. In mental health services this can be seen in the increasing structuring of services around diagnostic categories. In most geographic areas there are examples of such structuring which can include services for 'mild to moderate difficulties' – the latest example being the government-driven Improving Access to Psychological Therapies (IAPT) project (Department of Health, 2007) – services for severe and enduring mental illness, services for psychosis, eating disorders and personality disorders, to name but a few. Both pharmaceutical and psychological therapy interventions applied within these services are then dictated by NICE guidelines to be 'targeted' towards the particular 'symptoms' of that diagnostic category, as outlined in the *DSM-IV-TR* (*Diagnostic and Statistical Manual of Mental Disorders,* 4th ed, text rev) (American Psychiatric Association, 1994) and/or the *ICD-10* (*International Statistical Classification of Diseases and Related Health Problems,* 10th rev) (World Health Organization, 1992). Thus diagnosis and 'treatment' have become increasingly entwined (see Gilbert & Shmukler, 2003) and services generally reflect this by using diagnostic criteria for inclusion and exclusion.

Advantages of the diagnostic system

Within mental health the diagnostic system is well established and has some advantages. For practitioners, when faced with the emotional needs of clients, some of whom may be in significant distress or threatening to hurt themselves or others, it can be extremely reassuring to know there is a supporting system in place which 'tells' the practitioner what they should 'do'. I clearly remember my own anxiety when I began training, a time when I felt particularly out of my depth, and I wished for some certainty in the form of answers about the 'right' way to 'cure' the client and thus remove the emotional pressure I was experiencing. The diagnostic system offers the hope of this by pointing the practitioner towards the relevant guideline for 'treatment' options.

For clients, who feel at the mercy of distressing emotions ('symptoms') that they are struggling to understand and cope with, it can also be reassuring to discover they are not as isolated as they perhaps feared; their experience is validated in that they belong to a group with a diagnostic name that implies there is a 'cure' in the form of the practitioner, assumed to be an expert, who will take care of things, manage the problem, and make it go away. I have had this reported to me many times in 'symptom management' type groups which I have facilitated, where clients have told me that they began to feel a little better once they had been accepted into a particular group, before the therapy had actually begun. For some, the generalised interventions aimed at managing 'symptoms' they then received allowed them to feel more able to deal with that which had previously felt unmanageable.

The attractiveness of such a system may also go beyond practitioners and their clients, however, to operate at a more societal level. The pressures upon mental health services to implement 'neat', 'tidy' diagnoses and related interventions quite possibly underlie the hope that in doing so this will 'rid' us of the difficult emotional aspects in wider society that we find too 'messy', disturbing, perhaps violent or unmanageable (Holmes, 1999).

Arguably then, the diagnostic system offers clients, practitioners, and society as a whole, a common reassurance that implicitly promises the support of the collective when confronted with distressing emotional issues, alongside the hope that it will offer a route to their understanding and removal. Whether these assumptions are realistic or not, the very real feelings of relief and security that the system might bring are not to be dismissed lightly considering the despair and hopelessness that can often accompany such issues. With this in mind, one might go on further to argue that without some kind of structure like this to offer emotional containment (whether it be a diagnostic system or not) it may not be possible even to begin to manage the demands placed upon mental health services.

Disadvantages of the diagnostic system

Despite the benefits of the diagnosis system, however, it is equally frustrating, unsatisfactory and restricting in practice. Many of the clients with whom I have worked reported that no single diagnosis, or combination of diagnoses, fully captured their situation. They felt significantly different from others with the same diagnosis, and thus referral for specialist interventions, regardless of any initial hopefulness, seemed not fully to meet their needs. For these clients, dealing with their 'symptoms' alone proved inadequate and they reported that they continued to struggle with their distress during or after the end of therapy, which led many of them back into services.

As a clinical example of a client for whom diagnosis proved unsatisfactory, I am reminded of a young woman I worked with who had received a diagnosis of obsessive-compulsive disorder (OCD). She told me that she had then been referred for a therapy that had aimed to target the 'symptoms' of her OCD – in particular anxiety around making decisions, and the way that she coped with this by relying on a seemingly arbitrary 'ritualistic' system of checking the time of day. She said that this system gave her both comfort if she followed it and anxiety that something 'bad' would happen if she did not. She said the practitioner had suggested that her problem was due to an automatic pattern of negative thinking about herself that lowered her confidence and heightened her anxiety about her ability to manage decisions. The practitioner had suggested techniques she could use to challenge these thoughts and lessen her reliance on rituals in the hope that this combination would break the negative cycles she found herself in. It was believed that, with practice, this would demonstrate to her that she could manage. Her experience, however, was that challenging her thinking and behaviour had not alleviated the emotional distress she struggled with and thus her difficulties had not gone away.

Although this young woman's 'symptoms' may have suggested that it was entirely appropriate to cluster and treat her in the same way as others who have received a diagnosis of OCD, her individual story was important. This woman said to me that her family had expected her to be self-reliant from quite a young age. As many children do, she had tried to meet these expectations in order to avoid disapproval. Despite her efforts, overwhelming, but understandable, age-appropriate fears she was left feeling unable to manage this and she had relied on rituals to help her make decisions as far as possible rather than risk disapproval by sharing her emotional needs with her family. In her case, holding rigidly to a diagnosis and 'symptom'-focused intervention played into her belief that she was expected to be able to cope with everything alone once she had been taught these techniques, and this increased her fear of disapproval if she 'failed'. Whilst the diagnosis might have initially offered comfort in the form of an 'expert' who might 'remove' her fear and fulfil her wish to be able to cope with absolutely everything alone, unsurprisingly this was never going to be possible. Instead, the certainty and rigidity of this approach had placed the power with the practitioner, leaving little space to consider that the client might need a different approach within which she could challenge her assumption that she should be entirely self-reliant. Thus this client had left therapy as she had come in, i.e. unable to share her struggles and recruit others to support her in an appropriate manner.

The poor outcome described in the example above, and many others like it, have led practitioners to a growing concern about the risks of using a diagnostic way of working. In particular, there are concerns that diagnosis, and the related application of standardised therapies to target 'symptoms', can wrongly assume that this accurately captures the needs of the individual. Actually, in a world that is becoming increasingly standardised (or 'McDonaldized' as Ritzer, 1993 puts it), Foulkes and Anthony (1965) argue that many are brought to mental health services in the first place because they have been historically unable to get their individual needs recognised and met against such socially imposed norms. Brandchaft and Stolorow (1984) warn us that for some, to replicate this in imposing a diagnosis and standardised 'treatment', without acknowledging the impact this way of being has on them, is likely to increase their emotional distress rather than decrease it. Paradoxically then, this not only traps the client but also the practitioner into a given way of understanding emotional distress within which they cannot see how their, and society's, way of being contributed to the development and reinforcement of the problem. Frustratingly, this disempowers both practitioner and client, limiting their awareness of alternative possibilities and their ability to make choices in a manner that is meaningful and right for them. As Yalom puts it, this is 'denying the freedom and responsibility that I, as an individual, hold … [because I am] falling in with the crowd,' (1980: 24), or, in this case, falling in with the diagnosis and related intervention, which are taken as a 'given' rather than as plastic and contingent. This can then lead to heightened distress, repeat presentations and endless onward referrals. In some really unfortunate cases, this frustration can lead to inappropriate, 'hidden' blame which can then make matters worse for the client, e.g. clients described as 'treatment resistant', 'not trying', and/or 'difficult'.

Beyond diagnosis

As most clients are given a diagnosis to gain access to mental health services in the good faith that this will lead to the most 'effective treatment', it is extremely unfortunate that this, and the related standardised interventions that follow, can actually create a situation which reinforces that which underlies their distress in the first place. As has been argued, this is because a reliance on diagnostic thinking can inadvertently distance the practitioner from being able to discover the individual needs of the client, which thereby leads to an incomplete understanding of their emotional distress and 'treatments' which do not then tackle that which needs to be tackled. Whilst work is ongoing to promote less restrictive ways of working that might offer an alternative to the diagnostic system (see Neimeyer & Raskin, 2000), the system is dominant, extremely well established, and many rely on it to provide them with the certainty, hope, and reassurance they feel they need. To challenge the system would be to threaten the implicit containment it brings, raising the possibility of high levels of distress that many would feel unable to accept, particularly when there is the potential for physical harm. Some might argue that in such cases, the priority is to enforce interventions that will subdue the client's distress, at least for a time, rather than allow it free expression that could result in potentially damaging behaviour. This perhaps explains why the system is still in place and so resistant to change, aside from a few additions and deletions to the diagnostic manuals in the hope that this will patch up the flaws (see Jarrett, 2011). It is highly unlikely, therefore, that health services will simply drop the diagnostic way of working and the challenge for practitioners is therefore to consider how to work within it, balancing the need to create 'a space where the client's story can be heard' (Cohn, 1997: 33), against the ongoing social pressure to provide standardised, 'symptom'-focused therapies.

In practice, I have discovered that things are not always 'either/or' and, at least at a local level, I have met many practitioners who recognise the importance of supporting more individualised work wherever possible. This can create some flexibility in the system and, whilst not ideal, this can be highly beneficial for some clients who are willing to engage in this way. To some degree the practitioner can then refrain from imposing standardised interventions on the client, instead encouraging and supporting the client to explore their own needs, through an unfolding process, within the sessions, and in the wider context of their lives. In practical terms, practitioners might still make use of standardised interventions, but cautiously, after careful consideration of whether or not the offering of these is in line with the client's emerging needs, and always suggesting that these are flexible and open to discussion, rather than concrete and fixed. It is hoped that this way of working then empowers and enables the client to begin to experience the therapeutic relationship as less characterised by the stereotypes of the diagnostic system, i.e. the imposition of standardised 'treatment', but more focused on creating a genuine dialogue that recognises the autonomy and uniqueness of the other and can be used to acknowledge and explore limitations and possibilities for wider choice and change (Spinelli, 1989).

For the young woman I used as an example earlier, working in a more individualised manner proved more satisfactory than her previous experiences within the diagnostic framework. During our initial meetings, having realised that trying to impose further 'techniques' upon her was not likely to succeed (as they had failed previously), I placed my faith in exploring what presented in our sessions instead. Initially she expressed anger at me for this stance, telling me that she expected me to have 'answers' for her. Exploration of this, however, led us to consider her assumptions that I (and everyone else) 'knew what they were doing' and would criticise her if she did not. Explicitly telling her that I did not have all the answers (and even if I did, they would be my answers and not necessarily be right for her), alongside expressing a more realistic commitment to work alongside her to understand her underlying needs and find her own answers to these, led her to form a different kind of working relationship with me. As our work continued, she stopped being so angry at me, less afraid that I would be critical of her for not knowing and more comfortable in knowing I would support her to talk about whatever felt important to her at the time. Together, we began to notice how her initial assumptions about me applied to other situations in her social life. However, she used the work she had done with me to begin to risk sharing some of her thoughts and feelings with others too. To her delight, many of them began to tell her about similar feelings about everyday events, allowing her to realise that her feelings were not the 'symptom' of some 'illness' but, like other people, no one had all the answers, and everyone required support at times. Her anxiety and reliance on rituals decreased as her support network blossomed, leaving her feeling that she no longer needed to rely upon me or mental health services anymore.

As can be seen in this example, clients can become distressed when answers are not given, sometimes aiming their feelings directly at the practitioner, as this can challenge that which they have come to expect. This can raise difficult emotions for the practitioner who then feels under pressure to 'make things better'. It may seem very tempting to try and provide standardised answers at such times, but practitioners should be wary about their motivation for offering these. To try to lessen the emotional pressure that the practitioner feels by subduing the client's distress risks perpetuating the very issues which underlie it. Difficult though it may be, the client's distress should be allowed to be expressed because it is a communication of need that should be recognised, not 'removed' (Casement, 1985). In the long run, this, alongside an empathic opportunity to explore the individual's needs demonstrates to the client that their emotions are not necessarily 'symptoms' of 'illness' that need 'removing', but valid and important. This challenges the client's passive reliance on the practitioner and service to provide a specialist answer whilst asserting instead that they can be empowered to learn how to identify and negotiate satisfactory solutions to their own unmet needs. Whilst empowering for the client, this way of working can also reduce the frustration of the practitioner in that there is no longer a pressure to be right and so restricted in their interventions. Instead, it offers the practitioner a framework to explore the complexities and difficult feelings that present within the therapeutic relationship, using these to gain a greater understanding of the client's emerging needs, and to work with the client on these in a more equal, creative, and ultimately satisfactory manner.

Conclusion

In describing the well-established diagnostic system I have argued that it is a standardised system that attempts to categorise types of human distress by 'symptoms'. I have suggested that this system has benefits for clients, practitioners and society in acting as a containing structure at times of high distress and in suggesting related interventions that aim to manage the 'symptoms' of the individual's distress. I have also argued that diagnosis is subjective, flexible, imperfect, subject to change and just one way of viewing human distress. However, if standardised ways of viewing and working with human distress are considered as a given, this can therefore bind us into ways of thinking, feeling and behaving that can reinforce the underlying issues that prevent the individual from meeting their needs. The challenge therefore, is somehow to balance the socially driven demands to implement standardised diagnoses and related interventions within mental health services against the need to foster a therapeutic relationship which provides a space where the client's individual needs can be supported and a more holistic perspective of the client's distress can be gained. This necessarily involves careful and sometimes difficult negotiations between the practitioner, client and the organisation, and it is not always possible to achieve a satisfactory resolution. However, as the following chapters demonstrate, in practice, a more individualised way of working is often valued by many and supported to some degree. When it is possible to work in this way, it can be empowering for both practitioner and client as they explore how the client might find more satisfactory ways to negotiate between their needs and the demands of society, rather than having continually to subdue them in favour of passively accepting the imposition of social norms (including diagnosis). This way of working requires the practitioner continually to reflect upon how and when their interventions are offered (rather than imposed), and whether there are better ways to encourage the client to find their own answers. This stance then permits a more useful consideration of the client's real needs, and, more importantly, may enable the client to feel more empowered to identify and meet their needs once the therapy has ended.

References

American Psychiatric Association (1994). *Diagnostic and Statistical Manual of Mental Disorders* (4th ed). Washington, DC: American Psychiatric Association.

Brandchaft, B & Stolorow, R (1984). The borderline concept: Pathological character or iatrogenic myth? In J Lichtenberg, M Bornstein & D Silver (Eds) *Empathy II*. Hillsdale, NJ: Analytic Press.

Care Quality Commission (2010). *Our Enforcement Policy*. Retrieved 31 July 2011 from http://www.cqc.org.uk/sites/default/files/media/documents/cqc_enforcement_policy_oct_2010.pdf

Casement, P (1985). *On Learning from the Patient*. London: Routledge.

Cohn, HW (1997). *Existential Thought and Therapeutic Practice: An introduction to existential psychotherapy*. Thousand Oaks, CA: Sage.

Department of Health (2007). *Improving Access to Psychological Therapies: Specification for the commissioner-led Pathfinder programme*. Retrieved 31 July, 2011 from http://www.dh.gov.uk/prod_consum_dh/groups/dh_digitalassets/@dh/@en/documents/digitalasset/dh_074600.pdf

Department of Health (2009). *The NHS Constitution*. Retrieved 31 July 2011 from http://www.dh.gov.uk/prod_consum_dh/groups/dh_digitalassets/documents/digitalasset/dh_093442.pdf

Foulkes, SH & Anthony, EJ (1965). *Group Psychotherapy: The psychoanalytic approach*. London: Penguin Books.

Gilbert, M & Shmukler, D (2003). Counselling psychology in context. In R Woolfe, W Dryden & S Strawbridge (Eds) *Handbook of Counselling Psychology* (2nd ed). London: Sage.

Holmes, J (1999). Foreword: Simplicity, complexity and applying the group-analytic approach. In B Barnes, S Ernst & K Hyde (Eds) *An Introduction to Groupwork: A group-analytic perspective*. Basingstoke: Palgrave Macmillan.

Jarrett, C (2011). Society's critical response to DSM-5. *The Psychologist, 24*(8), 566-7.

Neimeyer, RA & Raskin, JD (Eds) (2000). *Constructions of Disorder: Meaning-making frameworks for psychotherapy*. Washington, DC: American Psychological Association.

Ritzer, G (1993). *The McDonaldization of Society*. London: Pine Forge.

Spinelli, E (1989). *The Interpreted World: An introduction to phenomenological psychology*. London: Sage.

Strawbridge, S & Woolfe, R (2003). Counselling psychology in context. In R Woolfe, W Dryden & S Strawbridge (Eds) *Handbook of Counselling Psychology* (2nd ed). London: Sage Publications.

World Health Organization (1992). *International Statistical Classification of Diseases and Related Health Problems* (10th rev). Geneva: World Health Organization.

Yalom, I (1980). *Existential Psychotherapy*. New York: Basic Books.

2

Depression:
Un-medicalising misery

Joanna Jackson

Introduction

'Depression'[1] has always flummoxed me. I think that is because it raises questions which I find hard to answer. I have personal questions about what the difference is between my 'normal' experience of depression compared to those who have been given the diagnosis. I have professional questions about how such a bewildering array of life experiences give rise to one disorder and exactly how people diagnosed with depression differ from those who have another primary diagnosis (especially given that most of my clients experience 'depression', as is currently defined, in some form or other). And I have broader questions about why there are millions of people diagnosed with the disorder in the UK alone and why this number continues to increase.

My struggle to understand depression is nothing new. It was Seligman (1975) who first described 'depression' as the 'common cold of psychopathology; at the same time familiar and yet mysterious'. Indeed, depression is one of the most common psychiatric diagnoses, affecting over 300 million people today and predicted to be the second largest cause of death and disability in the world by 2020 (Commonwealth Department

---

1. The term 'depression' can carry very different meanings depending on how it is used and by who it is used. Rather than elaborating specific meanings each time the word is used, the reader should adopt a critical and questioning stance and read the chapter with a variety of meanings in mind as this chapter has to make reference to the experience of clients, of therapists and of a relatively static diagnostic template.

of Health and Aged Care, 2000; McLoughlin, 2002). It is therefore a diagnosis we are all likely to have come across: in our professional roles, within our social circles and in the public eye. It is not only the diagnosis that is familiar, but like the common cold, 'depression' also describes an affective state known to us all.

For all its familiarity, perhaps partly because of it, the precise nature and meaning of depression remains vague and elusive. Moreover, the current treatment of choice that is based on the diagnosis, cognitive behaviour therapy (CBT), does not seem to be having its desired effect. Despite the UK Government heavily investing in CBT to reduce depression rates (Department of Health, 2006), the numbers afflicted have continued to rise (Mental Health Foundation, 2010). What is it that we are missing?

While depression is clearly a complex issue, I propose that it is in the area of how we relate to one another that is fundamental to understanding and working with this form of human distress. This chapter explores this idea, beginning with a critique of the diagnosis, followed by a brief consideration of the importance of 'relating' to the cause and characterisation of depression. I will then offer a more extensive reflection on the significance and quality of the therapeutic relationship in helping individuals who are suffering in this way, under the ironic title of 'cure'. I will look at what hinders such a relationship and the impact that this type of relating has had on me personally. Clinical material will be used for illustrative purposes. However, identifying information has been omitted or altered and pseudonyms used to ensure client confidentiality and anonymity.

The diagnosis of depression

Not only does it seem prudent to begin by examining current mainstream understandings of 'depression', but it also provides a basis for considering alternative, more relational conceptualisations of this form of human distress. When exploring the psychiatric and psychological literature, we soon discover that a variety of opinions can be found as to what constitutes 'depression'. Not only have types and sub-types come in and out of fashion, but professional texts have assigned primacy to different core features (see Frances & Hall, 1991; Pilgrim & Bentall, 1999). For example, some have understood depression as a disturbance of mood (see Becker, 1977), whereas others characterise it by cognitive dysfunction, involving a negative view of the self, the world and the future (see Beck et al., 1979).

When considering the accepted psychiatric diagnosis of depression, the picture, in some ways, does not become much clearer. The two most widely established systems for classification are the *Diagnostic and Statistical Manual of Mental Disorders*, currently in its fourth edition (*DSM-IV*) (American Psychiatric Association, 1994) and the *International Classification of Diseases*, its tenth edition (*ICD-10*) (World Health Organization, 1992).

When discussing the development of the classification of depression in the *DSM-IV*, Frances and Hall describe the confusion concerning the number and type of symptoms required to justify the diagnosis. They concluded that there are 'multiple plausible solutions … none has sufficient available evidence (especially validity) to make the optimal choice obvious' (1991: 63). As a result, the *DSM-IV* portrays the disorder as a syndrome, requiring the presence of five symptoms to make the diagnosis. These symptoms must include depressed mood and/or loss of interest or pleasure, as well as any of the following:

- weight gain or loss
- insomnia or hypersomnia
- psychomotor agitation or retardation
- fatigue
- feelings of worthlessness or guilt
- diminished ability to concentrate or make decisions
- recurrent thoughts of death or suicidal ideation

The *ICD-10* suggests an even looser inclusion criterion, describing ten 'common symptoms' including:

- depressed mood
- loss of interest and enjoyment
- reduced energy
- tiredness after slight effort
- reduced concentration and attention
- reduced self-esteem and confidence
- ideas of guilt and unworthiness
- pessimistic views of the future
- ideas or acts of self-harm or suicide
- diminished appetite

All of the above may be present but none (including depressed mood or loss of interest/pleasure) are considered essential for the diagnosis (World Health Organization, 1992). Clearly, the extent to which symptoms of depression are present and the way in which they are combined is considerably variable. This could lead to the curious situation of two individuals, sharing no common symptoms, being given the same diagnosis (Mendels, 1970; Pilgrim & Bentall, 1999).

Benefits and limitations of diagnosis

Unsurprisingly, such diagnostic approaches have been severely criticised as providing no consistency about the necessary and sufficient criteria for depression (e.g. Cooper, 2004; Kendell & Jablensky, 2003; Pincus et al., 1998). Not only is it difficult to judge when depression should be classified as a 'mental disorder' rather than a normal part of human emotional functioning, but the boundaries are also blurred between depression and other diagnoses, such as anxiety, attachment and personality disorders (Casey et al., 2001; Richardson, 2006; Shorter & Tyrer, 2003). In fact, many argue that there is so much overlap between depression and anxiety that the two diagnoses should be abandoned in favour of a single pathological condition (Montgomery, 1990; Shorter & Tyrer, 2003).

While being mindful of its significant limitations, I am not intending to dismiss the diagnosis as entirely redundant. Indeed, there are both clients and clinicians who would attest to its value. In particular, the diagnosis provides some clients with a sense of relief by giving a name to their experience. With the name comes not only the hope that there might be an explanation and cure, but also a recognisable term to communicate their distress to family, friends, clinicians, colleagues and the government. Similarly, there are clinicians for whom the diagnosis provides a framework within which to work, for example by guiding decisions regarding protocol-based 'treatments' as well as enabling better communication with medical colleagues about shared patients.

Nevertheless, I would argue that the diagnosis as it stands is superficial at best, incoherent at worst, and could even be functioning as a catch-all phrase for individuals who are experiencing debilitating emotions, but who do not fit well into another category of diagnosis. Even if it is appropriate to group such a large number of individuals, who are potentially experiencing discretely different symptoms, depression certainly is not as clear cut or understood as the diagnosis implies.

On one level, this should also keep us wary of using the diagnosis as an explanation in itself and therefore invoking a tautological argument; as demonstrated by the following line of questioning:

Q: How do we know this patient is depressed?

A: Because they have a low mood and feel worthless.

Q: Why do they have a low mood and feel worthless?

A: Because they are suffering from depression. (Pilgrim, 2008: 261).

However, perhaps more importantly, such limitations with the diagnosis demand that we keep searching for a better understanding of depression, and in doing so, we remain alert to the ways in which the diagnosis may act as a barrier to a deeper, more nuanced understanding of human distress.

While there are many directions that one could take when striving to develop our understanding of human misery, it is the matter of human relating that, in my experience, has proven to be vital in appreciating, comprehending and offering something of therapeutic value to the person diagnosed with depression. The importance of relating and relationships is also something that is absent from the diagnosis. Therefore, the remainder of this chapter will be concerned with the centrality of human relating to the cause, characterisation and cure of depression. However, as we begin, I want to be clear that by focusing in on the issue of relating, I am not intending to reduce or restrict this very complex and nuanced issue to a singular factor. Instead, I hope the following discussion will serve to expand and stimulate further reflection, attention and insight into this human experience we call 'depression'.

The cause of depression: Relational discord

In one sense, depression has a multitude of causes. The histories of friends, family and clients I have worked with who suffer with depression are richly varied. The reasons (if any) they give for their misery are also diverse. Yet, what unites their diverse experience almost without exception is the issue of relational isolation or discord. As clients talk about what causes the depth of their suffering, they describe how it is not just the injustice they have faced, or the loss they have experienced, or the self-loathing they feel, but it is the fact that their suffering feels private and isolating which makes it so destructive and distressing. While it may be that we can think of people diagnosed with depression who we believe are far from alone or isolated, nevertheless, when it comes to human experience and interpersonal relating, there is an extent to which perception *is* reality, and this aloneness is most often the depressed person's reality.

It is not only anecdotal evidence from my clients' lives that suggests issues of relating and relationships are central to understanding the cause of depression. There is an extensive body of research demonstrating that depression can be meaningfully understood and predicted by the extent of an individual's relationships.

Research evidence

Neuropsychological studies have shown that an individual's early relationship with their primary caregiver provides the context within which important neural networks are shaped. These networks affect their ongoing attachment style, sense of safety and danger, as well as their core sense of self. A deficit or dysregulation of these neural networks has been shown to result in various emotional and social difficulties, including depression (Cozolino, 2010). It is therefore unsurprising that numerous studies into early attachment relationships demonstrate the close connection between the quality of early relationships and the likelihood of being diagnosed with depression in later life (see Ma, 2006).

It is not just early relationships that are significant; studies have also shown that depression can be meaningfully understood and predicted by the extent of an individual's relationships with people throughout their life. Moreover, other research has widened the focus even further by demonstrating that it is not only an individual's relationship with other people that is predictive of depression, but also their relationship with a higher being and/or the environment (see Hagerty & Williams, 1999; Morris, 1996; Vanderhorst & McLaren, 2005; Van Ness & Larson, 2002).

In addition to research evidence, the connection between depression and the quality of relationships is also indicated when considering socio-historical aspects.

Socio-historical evidence

When reviewing the prevalence of major depression in the Western world, it becomes clear that depression rates have significantly increased over recent years. In fact, people born after 1945 are ten times more likely to suffer with depression than those born before (Seligman, cited in Buie, 1988). Not only does this indicate that the primary cause of depression is not genetic, but raises questions about the impact that society has on the prevalence of depression.

Although many changes have occurred over the past five decades, some of the most apparent include a breakdown in immediate and extended family relationships, a dispersal of communities, and an increased focus on material wealth and 'the self' (Elliott & Tyrrell, 2003). All of these changes can be seen as having a potentially detrimental effect on the existence, establishment or maintenance of meaningful, reciprocal, personal relationships, thus creating a potent formula for depression.

The linkage between relationships and depression is further supported when we consider the type of societies where depression is virtually unknown; for example, in traditional Amish society in the US or the traditional Kaluli tribe of New Guinea. In these societies, kinship is a defining feature, individual concerns are synonymous to group concerns and relational support is integral to their way of life (Cross-National Collaborative Group, 1992). While we recognise these things to be valuable, this type of connection and collaboration is far rarer in our modern society. Depression, however, is more common.

Considering depression as having a relational cause is in contrast to the view of depression that the diagnosis presents, which locates the problem firmly with the individual. Therefore, not only does the diagnosis of depression overlook this potentially important cause, but it risks diverting us from socio-political factors that may be vital in responding to our clients' and our society's depression.

However, it is not only the centrality of relating to the cause of depression that is often overlooked in more medically orientated conceptualisations of this 'disorder'. The diagnosis also fails to consider that relating may be central also to the very nature, characterisation and essence of depression.

The characterisation of depression: Relational isolation

As I mentioned at the start, one of the questions that perplexes me about depression is what is the difference between being depressed and being unhappy? Or to put it another way, what is the difference between my clients' misery and the more ordinary and common experience of sadness?

Could the answer lie in this issue of relating? By this I mean that if you are unhappy, even if you have experienced the most terrible loss or struggle, you are still able to seek comfort from others. You can experience their sympathy, concern and love which, while it may not lift the sadness, does provide some sense of soothing, consoling or comfort. Whereas, if you are depressed, others' love, care or concern not only provides no solace, but often intensifies one's misery, thus creating a destructive cycle.

I remember one client describing how the efforts of others to encourage or cheer him were at best irritating, as he saw their comments as indicating that they did not understand or appreciate his experience. At worst, others' efforts only added to his deep sense of despair and dejection, as it reminded him how he could no longer gain any pleasure or connection from relationships. It was as if a wall existed between his world and the world of others, and he felt deeply alone in his depression.

Depictions and descriptions of depression

It seems that relational separation and seclusion is not only significant in understanding the cause of depression, but *is* the very essence of depression. For example, a therapist described the images that her depressed clients had drawn at the beginning of therapy to portray their feelings. They included: a person alone in a fog, an empty landscape or sea, a person alone and held down by a heavy weight or wrapped tightly in something, and a person trapped and abandoned. While some appear more hopeful than others, she noted that they all have one thing in common: 'The person is enduring terrible isolation' (Rowe, 1983: 3).

This sense of aloneness is also present in the verbal descriptions that depressed people give of their suffering. For example, Dominian records one forty-year-old woman's words: 'The aloneness that one goes through in depression is a kind of anguish. *Depression is being alone*, in darkness, in pain, in despair – and being unable to move one way or the other' (1976: 20). Not only is depression marked *by* aloneness, but this sufferer depicts depression *as* aloneness. In this way, depression can be seen as fundamentally a relational issue, both in cause and characterisation, and this points to the importance of relating and relationships in addressing depression. So, it is here that we come to the turning point of the chapter as we begin to consider the implications that our discussion has thus far for therapeutic practice and, in particular, the therapeutic relationship.

The 'cure' for depression: Relational connection

There is a vast body of research which demonstrates the importance and significance of the therapeutic relationship in any effective therapy. For example, studies have confirmed that it is the therapeutic alliance, more than any other variable, including the therapeutic model and technique, which most closely relates to outcome (e.g. Lambert, 2007; Parker & Fletcher, 2007; House & Loewenthal, 2008). To proclaim the importance of the therapeutic relationship, therefore, is not novel. However, given the centrality of relating to the cause and characterisation of depression, there is something perhaps uniquely special and necessary about the therapeutic relationship when working with someone suffering in this way.

On the basis of clients' descriptions that isolation is central to the experience of depression, one of my main aspirations as a therapist is to attempt to bridge the expanse between our worlds with the hope that this connection might bring some comfort. Within therapy, this connection may come in a variety of forms, including having a shared understanding of their difficulties and collaborating on the general purpose as well as specific goals for therapy. But, in addition, or perhaps even more fundamentally, I would argue that therapeutic connection comes through the therapist inwardly resonating with the client's experience. This is more than the therapist simply obtaining an intellectual appreciation of a client's problem. It is primarily co-feeling, co-understanding and co-experiencing something of their inner lives (Watkins, 1978). It is on this basis that a verbal understanding can then be co-constructed.

While this type of relationship is given more or less precedence depending on the type of therapy, it nonetheless exists in all therapies (Gelso & Carter, 1985). For example, within the humanistic tradition, it is described as the 'person-to-person' relationship (Clarkson, 2003); within Gestalt therapy there is similarly an emphasis on full and genuine engagement between patient and therapist (Jacobs, 1989); within the psychoanalytic tradition there is acknowledgement of the role of the real relationship alongside the transference/counter-transference relationship (Hamilton, 1982); and within existential therapy there is also recognition of the importance of the present emotional relationship that exists between client and therapist (Yalom, 1980).

As well as long-standing therapies acknowledging the value and necessity of developing this type of relationship, recent developments within the field of neuropsychology have also provided empirical confirmation of the value of such relational connection. In particular, neuroscience has shown that the way we bring ourselves fully into connection with our clients is one of the most powerful determinants of a positive outcome of psychotherapy (Norcross et al., 2005). Moreover, it is by the therapist creating an environment that maximises the positive neurochemistry of attachment through human compassion and emotional attunement, in combination with language, that neural circuitry can be stimulated to grow in ways which are healing (Cozolino, 2010). In this way, therapy becomes an experience of mutual engagement and empathy, which is grounded in human authenticity and affinity.

Despite the widespread recognition and evidence of the value of this type of relating between therapist and client, I have found that it does not come easily, especially when working with the experience of depression. There are significant barriers to relating, both from the perspective of the client as well as the therapist.

Barriers to relating: Client's disconnection

From the perspective of the client, there is frequently a monotonous numbing that overshadows a more acute emotional discomfort, and just as their pain is cut off, so are we. Correspondingly, as therapists we often experience the relational disconnection that seems central to the aetiology of their distress. Even when there is an objective desire for connection (as is the case when a person requests therapy and understands that this entails meeting with someone to share and work through their difficulties), it is the cry of 'Help me, help me – stay away' that often sums up my experience of the therapeutic relationship.

Monica

By way of illustration, I wish to introduce you to Monica – a client who taught me much about patient disconnection and the struggle for relational connection. Monica was in her early 40s, single and working as an administrator within a large company. She had suffered a number of traumatic losses in her life, including the death of her father when she was a child, followed by sexual abuse for a number of years, and more recently the death of two siblings in a terrorist bombing. She reported suffering from recurrent depressive disorder since her teenage years and difficulty in forming relationships of any kind. For a number of years, she had managed to keep her depression hidden from friends, family and work colleagues. However, recently she had experienced a worsening in symptoms, explaining that she could no longer 'keep up the mask' and found herself unable to continue with work or other daily activities.

I first met with Monica whilst working within a psychoanalytic psychotherapy unit. Before being referred to our service, Monica had tried a number of previous interventions unsuccessfully, including various forms of medication, individual CBT and group therapy. Following assessment, I contracted to meet with Monica once a week for one year.

For this year of therapy, Monica attended every session, never missing an appointment and always arriving a few minutes early. In this sense, she was keen and diligent to engage therapeutically with me. However, in sessions Monica would refuse to talk about her painful experiences or emotions, she would criticise therapy and express frustration at me for not giving her what she needed to no longer feel depressed. At other times she would not say anything, choosing to sit in silence, waiting until our time ended, at which point she would ask with a contemptuous tone: 'Can I go now?' I was shut out from her world and given clear signals that she did not want me to intrude.

During sessions I would feel a wide variety of emotions: hopelessness, helplessness, irritation, anger, as well as heartbreaking sadness. I was frustrated that she did not want to relate to me, to confide in me or to connect with me. I frequently found myself wanting to give up on trying to form a relationship with her, either by withdrawing, pushing her away through unsupportive comments and interpretations, or simply suggesting that we terminate the therapeutic contract early. Every session felt like an internal, but very real fight to remain open, emotionally available and to continue striving to connect. After sessions, I would feel exhausted and emotionally bruised. On the one hand I wanted to protect myself from this experience by erecting an invisible wall between myself and Monica and make a decision not to care or let her affect me. On the other hand, I was sure that to do so would not be therapeutic, helpful or healing for her, and as long as she did not give up coming to therapy, I too must not give up being therapeutic, as far as I knew how.

With the support of my supervision group, I was able to conceptualise the potential meaning and purpose of our relationship in theoretical and therapeutic terms, nevertheless, there seemed to be little fruit from our sessions. As therapy progressed in much the same fashion, I wondered whether it was helping at all and felt very despondent about the actual value of our relationship. In the sessions leading up to the ending, I tried to explore with Monica her thoughts and feelings about the end. Her only response was to reassure and remind me that, given she did not get anything of worth from our sessions, she was looking forward to not having to come anymore. I began to resign myself to the fact that while this therapeutic experience seemed not to have been helpful for the client, it had at least developed my own therapeutic strength! Our final session was once again spent largely in silence, despite my attempts to reflect on the past year of therapy and what her next step might be. When our time was up, I told Monica we had come to the end of our session and as usual, she got up from the chair, put on her coat and opened the door. But then something very unusual and unexpected happened. As she stepped out of the room she turned to me and said 'I don't know what has changed, I doubt it is therapy that has helped, but I don't feel depressed anymore'. Then she left.

In one sense, for the duration of therapy, Monica remained disconnected. By the end of a year's therapy, I knew no more about Monica's history, her daily activities, her relationships, her desires or her thoughts than I did following assessment. We experienced no warm, comfortable or pleasurable moments of intimacy. Even when she was in my presence, the sense was that she remained painfully alone, almost unable to speak or relate to me as another human being. However, from another perspective, she communicated to me more of what she felt than words could have ever achieved. Through our encounter I gained a felt sense of what her struggle with depression was like – the anger, the hopelessness, the sadness, the fight. I got to know her from the inside out and in this sense we achieved a type of connection; it was real, I was affected, and our relationship was ultimately therapeutic.

My experience with Monica was a vivid example of the disconnection that often marks therapeutic work with a depressed person. It is also a testament to the value of persistence and perseverance in forming a therapeutic connection. However, it is not just the client's disconnection that interferes with therapeutic relating; therapists too are in danger of our own form of relational disconnection.

Barriers to relating: The therapist's disconnection

With Monica, as with other clients who are suffering with depression, relational therapy involves the witnessing and partaking of another's suffering. Regardless of whether the overriding emotion is one of anger, sadness or disorientation, it is always deeply uncomfortable, if not actually painful, and my own reactive desire is often to avoid this experience. Such avoidance can come in many forms. With Monica, it was shown in my desire to withdraw or retaliate. With other clients, it can manifest in ambivalence and apathy. However, an even more subtle and curious manifestation of avoidance can present in the urge to hasten the cure; and this is, perhaps, the most dangerous form of avoidance, precisely because of its subtlety.

As a therapist, I have a desire, indeed obligation, to work as effectively as I can for my clients' well-being. Nevertheless, I have become aware of the danger of trying to fast-forward the therapeutic process by providing quick-fix solutions, not because this is what is called for, but because it provides a way of avoiding and bypassing clients' painful emotions. However, such 'quick fixes' are often ineffective (at least in the long term), if not actually antitherapeutic, and usually impede the forming of a genuine connection. Let me develop this further by way of a personal example.

Clare

I have a friend, Clare, whom I have known for many years. We have a similar background, are at a similar stage of life, have similar interests and current circumstances. However, Clare has been diagnosed as suffering from long-term depression but I have not. At times when she has felt low, she has often described to me the sadness that she feels, the uncontrollability and unpredictability of her emotions, her inability to experience pleasure or peace and her sense of loneliness.

As Clare describes to me her distress, I experience a repeated pattern of reactions: on one level, I feel guilty; guilty that she is suffering when I am not; that her life seems to feel like a battle and mine does not; that she experiences so much pain, when I do not: guilty that I am different. On another level, I feel fearful. Fearful that underneath it all, I am the same; that it is only by denying and disowning my vulnerable, needy and dysfunctional parts that I am not experiencing the very same struggle and anguish that she is, and therefore, at any moment I too might be afflicted by the same 'dis-ease'.

It is from these (often sub-conscious) reactions of fear and guilt that I long to escape. So rather than allowing myself to co-feel, co-understand and co-experience something of her distress, I am driven to find a 'quick-fix', longing to get rid of this dangerous 'depression' as swiftly as possible. Rather than listening to her, I begin to suggest various ways she might be able to change her circumstances or reframe her experience, trying to convince her that things are not as bad as they seem. But no matter what solutions I come up with, our conversations usually end with my friend feeling unheard and unhelped and me feeling frustrated and confused.

I use this example, not primarily to comment on the methods of change I was attempting to utilise in my conversation with Clare. After all, changing circumstances and reframing thoughts often have their place when working therapeutically with depression. Instead, I believe the reason why my efforts were untherapeutic was largely because they were attempted in absence of a relational connection. My own emotional reaction of anxiety and guilt got in the way of co-feeling, co-understanding and co-experiencing something of her inner life. While this can perhaps be forgiven as I am her friend, not her psychologist and it is a personal relationship, not a professional one, nevertheless, I believe this same cycle of events can also occur in the therapeutic relationship.

When faced with someone suffering significantly with depression, rather than allowing, abiding and accepting the person's suffering alongside them, I am in danger of becoming very active in therapy, using all the psychological tools and techniques I have at my disposal to rid the person of their problem emotions. I can take the role of motivational coach or cheerleader: enthusiastically reciting well-rehearsed mantras in the form of therapeutic tools or techniques, all of which I do from the sidelines of their suffering. Again, I am not suggesting that there is never a place for such activity; only that such an approach can be used as a way of distancing and disconnecting, which consequently hinders the development of a genuine, authentic and mutual relationship and therefore undermines and impedes the therapeutic endeavour.

However, it is not just a desire to avoid sharing in another's distress that drives me to hasten the 'cure'. I also have a fear of what the depression might do to the sufferer. Not only does the diagnosis of depression recognise that a core feature is the sufferer experiencing recurrent thoughts of suicide, if not actual attempts, the Mental Health Foundation estimates that approximately 70 per cent of recorded suicides are committed by people experiencing depression (1997). It is a sad fact that, at least for some sufferers, experiencing depression is potentially life-threatening. When viewed from this angle, it surely seems prudent to 'hasten the cure'? What is more, within the pressure and stress of NHS systems, it is understandably hard to conceive responding to depression in any other way than to eradicate symptoms as quickly as possible. However, I do believe that there is a more fruitful, albeit, controversial angle to consider.

The risky value of depression

While it is true that too late an intervention can cost a life, I would also argue that too hasty an intervention may deprive the individual of a necessary experience in life; and in between these two poles lies a range of suffering which may have as much potential for good as it does for being destructive and wasteful (Dominian, 1976). This continuum, therefore, must be judged carefully. As mental health professionals, a thorough and ongoing risk assessment should always be an important part of our therapeutic work with those suffering with depression. Moreover, as I suggest that the experience of depression has the potential for good, I am mindful that I am in no way intending to undermine or neglect the terrible suffering that those diagnosed with depression face. Rather, I am suggesting that depression does often have a purpose in providing opportunity to grow, learn and change. As Philip Toynbee acknowledged when describing his own experience of depression:

> partly through [a] slow and heavy process within my mind and heart, I gradually began to think of this depression in quite a new set of terms. [...] I couldn't and still can't tell whether God sends us such acute afflictions to bring us to some new understanding through our pain. But I am now as sure as I can be that depression is often a sign, whether human or divine, that the life of the victim needs to be drastically changed. (1981: 56)

In my experience, both personal and professional, change such as this is often set in motion by the sufferer searching for answers to their suffering. Although some come to therapy only wanting relief from their symptoms, there comes a point at which most people begin to long to make sense of their suffering. After all, depression, perhaps more than any other diagnosis, begs the question 'why?' In contrast to anxiety for example, which typically asks 'when?' or 'how?', the depressed individual longs to know 'why did this happen to me?', 'why did he leave?', 'why did she abuse me?', 'why am I so unlovable?', 'why did my life turn out this way?' And even if these questions are not asked explicitly, they nevertheless pervade the therapeutic encounter, forming the tacit content of the work and affecting the shared experience of the relationship.

Whether asked explicitly or implicitly, these 'why?' questions cannot help but drive us back to the basic questions of life, meaning and purpose. Rarely do we allow time to reflect on these existential questions and I believe we are poorer as individuals, indeed as a society, because of this. But more to the point, it is through considering these existential questions that our 'whys?' become 'what?' as we ask ourselves 'what can I learn from this experience?' and more specifically, 'what can I learn about myself, about my relationships, about my life and about what needs to change?' Excitingly, if such reflection is allowed, therapy becomes a means of not only removing symptoms, but of actively enhancing life.

When considered from this perspective, our role as practitioners therefore, is not solely to provide a cure for their symptoms, but to walk alongside our clients in the midst of their distress, encouraging them to discover the answers to questions raised by their depression. In doing so, our aim is not simply that their life would return to 'normal', but that their life might be 'drastically changed' for the better.

Allowing room for such questions to be considered is not only therapeutically valuable in itself, but also serves the purpose of deepening the therapeutic relationship and connection. Because whilst we may not have experienced any of the same past atrocities, hurts or losses that our clients have, and while we may not share the same present pain, numbness or isolation that they feel, nevertheless these existential questions draw us together in our own humanity. They remind us that we indeed share in a fundamental likeness and therefore we can co-feel, co-understand and co-experience something of their struggles, because they are in fact our struggles. And in doing so, we can connect: genuinely, meaningfully, authentically and thus, therapeutically.

Widening our gaze

Depression remains a profoundly complex and common form of human distress that concerns not only individuals, but society in general, and we clearly still have a long way to go in understanding and effectively addressing this dis-ease. I have argued that one crucial aspect, which is often overlooked, is the issue of relating and relationships. The centrality of relating has profound implications for the way we seek to address depression, both from the perspective of mental health policy makers as well as mental health practitioners; and as I conclude, I want to draw our attention to some such implications.

As mentioned at the beginning, the government's current approach to address depression is to increase the provision of CBT. However, given the importance of the therapeutic relationship in addressing depression, there is perhaps a danger in the promotion of this particular model of psychotherapy above other models. This is because it increases the risk of diverting attention from the centrality and significance of relationality in effective therapy (Pilgrim, 2008). Moreover, CBT is also an approach that can be structured and manualised and therefore, it is perhaps easier to attend to techniques over and above the relationship within this model.

The dominance of CBT as the recommended treatment for depression is unlikely to change whilst randomised controlled trials (RCTs) are still deemed to be the gold standard for evaluating therapeutic interventions. The problem is that RCTs struggle to assess the quality of relational connection between therapist and client. Consequently, there is also the need to develop process and relational research approaches, which would be likely to provide a more valid and representative evidence base for 'best practice' recommendations for addressing depression (Barlow et al., 2004).

Considering the centrality of human relating within depression not only has implications for the type of therapy which is endorsed, but also to our whole approach in addressing depression. Reconceptualising our view of depression as an issue belonging to our society, rather than just the individual, opens up many other avenues for addressing depression, which may not come in the form of increasing access to psychological therapies. Instead, such possibilities could include voicing a challenge to modern consumerism and hedonistic materialism, which often result in the undermining of relationships, mutuality and social solidarity (Layard, 2005); or investing in socio-cultural initiatives to strengthen community, family, spirituality and so on.

Addressing depression within these broader spheres does not have be left up to politicians and policy makers. As clinicians, we too can be encouraged to think creatively with our clients about possibilities for addressing depression beyond the therapeutic relationship. For example, we could consider innovative ways of enhancing interpersonal relatedness within an individual's social contacts, environment and spiritual spheres of life. Regardless of what form such possibilities take, it seems prudent to become increasingly sensitive and attentive to the broader social forces impacting on the development, maintenance and recovery from depression.

I have argued that, at least within the psychotherapeutic context, it is the therapeutic relationship that holds great potential for restoration, remediation and recuperation. A therapeutic relationship that is based on co-feeling, co-understanding, co-experiencing and therefore 'co-nnecting' will profoundly alter the experience of depression. As we walk in the shadow of their path, clients will sense that they are no longer alone. A therapeutic relationship, which allows the emergence of questions that have thus far gone unanswered, will stimulate the potential of depression as a means of enhancing life. In our struggle with depression, I am convinced that it is through this simple yet profound and basic yet fundamental human relationship that there can emerge hope for the present and even optimism for the future.

References

American Psychiatric Association (1994). *Diagnostic and Statistical Manual of Mental Disorders* (4th ed). Washington, DC: American Psychiatric Association.

Barlow, DH, Allen, LB, & Choate, ML (2004). Toward a unified treatment for emotional disorders. *Behavior Therapy, 35,* 205–30.

Beck, AT, Rush, AJ, Shaw, BF & Emery, G (1979). *Cognitive Therapy of Depression.* New York: Guilford Press.

Becker, J (1977). *Affective Disorders.* Morristown, NJ: General Learning Press.

Buie, J (1988) 'Me' decades generate depression: Individualism erodes commitment to others. *APA Monitor, 19,* 18.

Casey, P, Dowrick, C & Wilkinson, G (2001). Adjustment disorders: Fault line in the psychiatric glossary. *British Journal of Psychiatry, 179,* 479–80.

Clarkson, P (2003). *The Therapeutic Relationship* (2nd ed). London: Whurr Publishers.

Commonwealth Department of Health and Aged Care (2000). *National Action Plan for Depression.* Canberra: Mental Health and Special Programs Branch.

Cooper, R (2004). What is wrong with the *DSM? History of Psychiatry, 15,* 5–25.

Cozolino, L (2010). *The Neuroscience of Psychotherapy: Healing the social brain.* New York: WW Norton & Co.

Cross-National Collaborative Group (1992). The changing rate of major depression: Cross-national comparisons. *JAMA, 268,* 3098–105.

Department of Health (2006). *Mental Health Bill.* London: Department of Health.

Dominian, J (1976). *Depression: What is it? How do we cope?* London: Fontana/Collins.

Elliott, R & Tyrrell, M (2003). *Depression: Understand it, treat it, beat it.* Retrieved January

28, 2011, from www.clinical-depression.co.uk/dlp/depression-information/medical-causes-of-depression/

Frances, A & Hall, W (1991). Work in progress on the *DSM-IV* mood disorders. In JP Feighner & WF Boyer (Eds) *Diagnosis of Depression.* New York: Wiley.

Gelso, CJ & Carter, JA (1985). The relationship in counselling and psychotherapy: Components, consequences, and theoretical antecedents. *The Counselling Psychologist, 13*(2), 155–243.

Hagerty, BM & Williams, RA (1999). The effects of sense of belonging, social support, conflict and loneliness on depression. *Nursing Research, 48*, 215–19.

Hamilton, V (1982). *Narcissus and Oedipus: The children of psychoanalysis.* London: Routledge & Kegan Paul.

House, R & Loewenthal, D (2008). *Against and for CBT: Towards a constructive dialogue?* Ross-on-Wye: PCCS Books.

Jacobs, L (1989). Dialogue in gestalt theory and therapy. *Gestalt Journal, 8*(1), 25–37.

Kendell, R & Jablensky, A (2003). Distinguishing between the validity and utility of psychiatric diagnoses. *American Journal of Psychiatry, 160,* 4–12.

Lambert, M (2007). What we have learned from a decade of research aimed at improving psychotherapy outcome in routine care. *Psychotherapy Research, 17,* 1–14.

Layard, R (2005). *Happiness: Lessons from a new science.* London: Penguin.

Ma, K (2006). Attachment theory in adult psychiatry. Part 1: Conceptualisations, measurement and clinical research findings. *Advances in Psychiatric Treatment, 12,* 440–9.

McLoughlin, G (2002). Is depression normal in human beings? A critique of the evolutional perspective. *International Journal of Mental Health Nursing, 11,* 170–3.

Mendels, J (1970). *Concepts of Depression.* New York: Wiley.

Mental Health Foundation (1997). *Briefing No. 1: Suicide and deliberate self-harm.* London: Mental Health Foundation.

Mental Health Foundation (2010). New Government figures reveal the economic burden of depression has risen to £9bn a year [Press release: 22nd November].

Montgomery, S (1990). *Anxiety and Depression.* London: Livingstone.

Morris, LE (1996). A spiritual well-being model: Use with older women who experience depression. *Issues in Mental Health Nursing, 17,* 439–55.

Norcross, J, Levant, R & Beutler, L (2005). *Evidence-based Practices in Mental Health: Debate and dialogue on the fundamental questions.* Washington, DC: American Psychological Association.

Parker, G & Fletcher, K (2007). Treating depression with the evidence-based psychotherapies: A critique of the evidence. *Acta Psychiatrica Scandinavica, 115,* 352–9.

Pilgrim, D (2008). Reading 'happiness': CBT and the Layard thesis. In R House & D Loewenthal (Eds) *Against and for CBT: Towards a constructive dialogue?* Ross-on-Wye: PCCS Books.

Pilgrim, D & Bentall, R (1999). The medicalization of misery: A critical realist analysis of the concept of depression. *Journal of Mental Health, 8*, 261–74.

Pincus, HA, Zarin, DA & First, M (1998). 'Clinical significance' and *DSM-IV. Archives of General Psychiatry, 55*, 1145–8.

Richardson, P (2006). The Layard proposals: A brief analysis. *Psychotherapy Section Review, 41*, 23–7.

Rowe, D (1983). *Depression: The way out of your prison.* London: Routledge & Kegan Paul.

Seligman, MEP (1975). *Helplessness: On depression, development and death.* San Francisco: Freeman.

Shorter, E & Tyrer, P (2003). Separation of anxiety and depressive disorders: Blind alley in psychopharmacology and classification of disease. *British Medical Journal, 327,* 158–60.

Toynbee, P (1981). *Part of a Journey: An autobiographical journal, 1977–1979.* London: HarperCollins.

Vanderhorst, RK & McLaren, S (2005). Social relationships as predictors of depression and suicidal ideation in older adults. *Aging and Mental Health, 9*, 517–25.

Van Ness, PH & Larson, DB (2002). Religion, senescence and mental health: The end of life is not the end of hope. *American Journal of Geriatric Psychiatry, 10*, 386–97.

Watkins, JG (1978). *Two Hands of God.* London: Rider.

World Health Organization (1992). *ICD-10: International Statistical Classification of Diseases and Related Health Problems* (10th rev). Geneva: World Health Organization.

Yalom, I (1980). *Existential Psychotherapy.* New York: Basic Books.

3

Anxiety: Reaching
through the fear

Lucy Atcheson

Defining anxiety

Having something to worry about occasionally is a normal part of life, but for some, worries develop into profound anxiety. This means relentless adrenaline pumping into the body, and constant recurring thoughts torturing the sufferer that all is not well and that doom or catastrophe is imminent. Moreover, they have the core belief that they are not capable of preventing, or coping with, any of it.

From a diagnostic point of view, 'anxiety' is very different from 'being anxious'. Anxiety comes about because of a belief that at every turn there is a threat to well-being. Sufferers feel unable to make decisions, to control their physiological reactions or thoughts, or to function properly. Due to this perceived inability to function, people struggling with anxiety doubt themselves, and furthermore they truly believe everyone else will doubt them too (Atcheson, 2008).

In some ways, anxiety can call a halt to people's lives. This sounds dramatic but if someone is endlessly worrying that they are not good enough at something they can become so preoccupied with this obsessive thought that it becomes a self-fulfilling prophecy. The thought literally takes up so much energy there is none left for action and the sufferer becomes even more convinced they are not good enough. They become trapped in a never-ending vicious circle; a downward spiral.

Those struggling with anxiety become bullied by overwhelming self-critical thoughts and doubts that echo endlessly in their minds. This is more than mere worry; anxiety is an everyday human fear manifested in extremis.

Fear is a natural human emotion, but the rationality of fear tends to be judged in relation to its specific context. When confronted with a herd of running elephants, most people would understand a fear reaction and empathise with the inevitable shortness of breath, extreme fight or flight compulsion, increased adrenaline, tunnel vision, humming in the ears, sweaty palms, and the inability to focus. However, the same understanding would not be offered to someone experiencing similar fear reactions on a crowded station platform. Whether it is a herd of elephants or a crowd of people, the fear can be the same and needs to be understood as such. There are different causes of fear for each individual.

Anxiety can be thought of as having four levels of intensity, the first is mild anxiety, which can generally be described, and experienced, as a sense of general uneasiness. The next level is persistent anxiety, a somewhat more disturbing and relentless feeling of uneasiness. This can increase into paranoia-inducing anxiety, which is experienced as the debilitating fear that something is going very wrong internally. The maximum point of anxiety can be described as acute panic – a never-ending sense of impending doom and a feeling of being completely incapable of doing anything about it (Atcheson, 2008).

What causes anxiety?

Cognitive behavioural theory and psychoanalytic studies offer insight into the cause of anxiety. These two approaches may address anxiety with different terminology, but they both contribute to our understanding and in some ways they both confirm our understandings.

Bowlby (1988) theorised that everyone interprets their world through internal working models. These facilitate internal scripts on which people base their interactions with others and the surrounding world. People struggling with anxiety tend to fixate on internal scripts that are based on self-doubt and fear.

Cognitive-behavioural theory reminds us that someone with anxiety has a continuous negative commentary running inside their head, like a relentless bully. This lowers self-esteem and causes increased self-doubt. Self-doubt then causes a lack of self-belief. Low self-belief means that the person develops destructive, yet accepted, core beliefs about themselves (core beliefs are analogous to Bowlby's concept of the internal working model). These core beliefs cause them to feel anxious about their capacity to manage their life, and the external world seems more difficult and problematic.

Anxiety symptoms

The symptoms for anxiety obviously vary from person to person. However, there are some presenting issues which seem to be synonymous with anxiety (Bourne, 2000).

Increased adrenaline is a common consequence of fear. Increased adrenaline prepares the body for the typical fear reaction, the compulsion to flee or respond aggressively – the fight or flight response. However, anxiety sufferers do not always want to fight or flee; they may be sitting at their desk trying to write a report, and so the increase in adrenaline is physiologically redundant and furthers the psychological distress. Moreover, anxiety is also linked to a sense of fear-based paralysis and this, coupled with increased adrenaline and a perceived inability to move, can result in extreme stress and even nausea and shortness of breath. Increased adrenaline also raises heart rate and can cause sweaty palms or blushing. This can result in the sufferer feeling even more self-conscious of their physical symptoms. Self-consciousness and embarrassment increase fear, stress, and self-dislike, resulting in low self-esteem and hypersensitivity to any perceived triggers. As the sufferer will be endlessly on guard against potential triggers, their thoughts can become obsessively negative. Negative recurring thoughts can lead to extreme pessimism about impending doom and maintain the experience of stress and the physical and psychological symptomology. This relentless self-doubt and increased adrenaline is constant so that the sufferer can't even get respite in sleep and can struggle with insomnia. The sufferer obviously wants to get rid of their symptoms but the anxiety causes them to believe that they need to 'solve' the stress rather than ignore it. This actually results in further collusion and intensification of the anxiety as there is the desire to be anxiety-free and a sense of urgency but with little effectiveness. The ineffectiveness is heightened by the absence of head-space for calm thinking.

There are many presenting issues and they are complicated to cope with. Anyone trying to cope with anxiety deserves understanding and respect for the psychological and practical complexity they have to deal with on a daily basis. The following case study illustrates the gradual, yet definite and destructive, transition from everyday stress into crippling fear with all of the symptoms mentioned above. The transition felt so overpowering that Clara felt out of control; that sense of helplessness resulted in her feeling hopeless.

Clara:[1] Disappointment develops into fear and anxiety

Clara was a career-driven 'twenty something' enjoying life to the full, when her relationship broke up and she was passed over for promotion. For one of the first times in her life she felt helpless to change a situation that she really did nor want and almost could not bear. She missed her partner, suffered loneliness, and did not want to give up her lovely flat, but as they rented it together she simply could not afford it by herself. Clara mourned all of the plans they had made that would never become reality and berated herself for working too hard and pushing him away.

A torturous, self-critical tirade began – she thought that she had been a 'bad' girlfriend because she prioritised work and this had got her nowhere, because even though it had been her main focus she had not been good enough for the promotion. Slowly this reccurring thought developed into the thought that she was not good enough professionally or personally; this escalated into the fear that she was a failure – and always would be. Her sense of failure kept her awake at night as she analysed her past to see what she could have done differently. This analysis was experienced as an endless tirade of criticism about what she had done wrong. So in the early hours of the morning, after not sleeping, as the sun was rising she lay exhausted and full of self-loathing, which more often than not caused a panic attack. For Clara almost every day started the same, with shortness of breath, sweaty palms, increased heart rate, fear of a heart attack, tears, panic, and the room spinning as she lay in her bed resenting life, herself and her helplessness.

Eventually Clara became entirely convinced that she was incapable of leading her life properly and that she was a laughing stock at work, that she would never hold down a relationship, was destined never to have a family and would always be alone. The drive and joy drained out of her life as she told herself she was incapable, with such conviction that she paralysed

---

1. In order to always protect confidentiality these case studies have been anonymised and all identifying features changed. They are not based on any one individual client, but are composite of many. Thus they are representative of 'anxiety' and not any one client in particular.

herself from attempting anything. She began to perceive life as a series of pass-or-fail scenarios and was utterly convinced that she was destined to fail. Such was the dramatic nature of her self-doubt that she began to fret about her ability to carry out the social interactions that she had previously breezed through, thereby increasing her sense of isolation. Furthermore she became self-conscious at the gym, feeling that she didn't really fit in and slowly but effectively all of the activities that had previously boosted her sense of worth vanished from her life. A relationship break-up, a job disappointment, everyday occurrences that happened simultaneously, literally knocked Clara off her feet and she landed on anxiety.

As we can read with Clara, anxiety can make the sufferer truly believe false core beliefs about their identity, which then massively undermine their self-esteem and capacity for self-belief (Bourne, 2000). Someone diagnosed with anxiety perceives and judges everything about themselves through a veil of that anxiety. This veil affects how they remember their past, more often than not manipulating memories into evidence of simply not being good enough. This apparent, but irrational, interpretation of the past profoundly and negatively affects their hopes for the future and therefore their ability to expect enjoyment and fulfilment in their future or even their present.

Development of core beliefs

We all engage in self-talk but with those who suffer from anxiety this self-talk is often negative and unhealthy. Specific external factors can contribute to an unhealthy relationship with the self, and the development of critical self-talk can also be unique. However, for the purpose of understanding and working with anxiety-induced core beliefs some universal principles need to be recognised.

Lack of self-belief is often caused by the messages received as a child. About the age of two, a child develops their own self-image based on looking into the face of their primary carer and seeing there how they are regarded through the smile and the glint in their primary carer's eyes (Bowlby, 1988). Because at such a young age the primary carer is of great importance, their opinion is absorbed and forms the foundation of self-belief. If the glint in the eyes and expression on the face radiate love, the child feels lovable and protected. If it is hard and cold the child feels unlovable and unsafe, but because young children are egocentric they believe this comes from a fault of their own. Furthermore, verbal criticism is absorbed as though true. The child does not question the primary carer's motives for criticism as they accept they are deserving of it. Thus someone else's pathologies and reasons to criticise the child become absorbed as the foundations for the child's core beliefs. Later on, a partner's abuse or a colleague's endless criticism can 'validate' those erroneous early beliefs so that the person being bullied blames themselves, feeling worthless and anxious about their own abilities. Destructive relationships have a greater negative impact because relationships with others are the most influential aspect of a person's life.

A traumatic experience – environmental or interpersonal – can be so overwhelming and threatening that the fear of it reoccurring causes profound anxiousness. This, coupled with self-loathing and thoughts about their inability to prevent the traumatic experience or protect themselves from it, can also develop into anxiety. And stress plays a part too. A certain degree of stress is a part of everyday life, but cumulative stress causes concern about the ability to cope. Over time, if there is no respite, this concern grows into chronic worry and self-doubt, and over a prolonged period, this everyday stress, coupled with self-doubt, can manifest as anxiety (Atcheson, 2008).

As with most psychological disorders, it seems that a blend of genetics and learnt behaviour causes a person to be vulnerable to anxiety at some point in their lives. Equally if they spend their developing years witnessing a parent respond anxiously to life, they will learn that life is terrifying, with certain interactions being completely overwhelming. Children turn to their carers to understand how to behave; if they are shown that the appropriate response is fear based, their behaviour and interactions with their world will mimic that.

Working with anxiety

Work with anxiety must focus on challenging self-criticism and rethinking destructive core beliefs. In my experience, the therapeutic paradigms perhaps most effective with anxiety tend to be integrative and pluralistic, incorporating aspects of cognitive behaviour therapy, the schema-focused approach (Padesky, 1994), client-centred therapy (Rogers, 1951), and developmental theories (Bowlby, 1951).

Cognitive behaviour therapy is based on the premise that cognitions, emotion, behaviour and physiology all affect each other. In relation to anxiety, the deep-rooted core beliefs cause the fear, the fear can lead to the anxious behaviours and avoidance, which in turn increase the negative self-criticism. This cements the belief that the false core beliefs are in fact true. Therefore, therapy needs to focus on understanding the nature and cause of the core beliefs, the properties of the self-criticism, and the environmental factors which make the sufferer vulnerable to self-doubt. The therapy, therefore has to focus on the person's past, present, and future expectations.

Schema-focused therapy helps by illuminating people's 'scripts' or 'stories' about themselves and their identity in relation to their world and how these interfere with their interaction with their world, and their relationship with themselves (Padesky, 1994).

To do the work of therapy a strong therapeutic relationship needs to be established (Gelso & Carter, 1985; Clarkson, 1995) which allows the client to feel safe enough to voice their fears. Rogers (1951) theorised that providing the necessary and sufficient therapeutic elements of empathy, unconditional positive regard, and congruence enabled the client to explore their distress. This atmosphere of safety and warmth can then be internalised by the client in the same way that a child can internalise the love of their primary carer (Meins, 1997). If the expression in the primary carer's eyes caused some of the self-doubt as described earlier in the chapter, this approach of providing unconditional positive regard would seem particularly useful in reversing the negative developmental experiences incorporated at an early age.

Once the client feels part of a strong working alliance (Gelso & Carter, 1985) they feel comfortable enough to explore their maximum point of pain (Hinshelwood, 1994). For those struggling with anxiety, this point will often relate to the main cause of their anxiety, i.e. their self-destructive core beliefs. Using circular and Socratic questioning (Padesky, 1994), the core beliefs can often be clearly defined and clarified collaboratively within the therapeutic relationship. These questioning techniques are crucial, but equally important is the art of listening to the answers. It is important for therapists not to assume that previous professional or personal experiences result in one's hypotheses about the core beliefs being unquestionably correct; accurate, non-judgemental, listening is essential.

Once core beliefs are defined, they can be challenged. Effective challenging often requires the client to be able to understand how these core beliefs developed. Even if, at first, this understanding is only theoretical, the more the person is able to reflect on past relationships and events that caused them to feel negative about themselves, the understanding will move from conceptual to experiential. If a person recognises that their thoughts are destructive and understands how they developed they will begin to feel differently about the permanence of the destructive, negative thought.

Insight into the causes of anxiety is also important as it often promotes the hope of change. This hope is often the first step to freedom from the fear. Once the client embraces hope they can support themselves in trying to control their anxious thoughts, challenge their self-criticism and change their behaviour. The techniques that are often associated with this therapeutic stage are critical self-thought diaries and challenging each self-criticism with positive mantras. These mantras can feel alien, or even ridiculous at the beginning, but with time and perseverance the client begins to become more familiar and therefore comfortable with positive self-talk (Padesky, 1994). The realisation that anxiety stems from their own thoughts, and therefore can be controlled by their own, albeit different, thoughts is often very helpful.

Challenging the internal bully and undertaking behaviour experiments that confront rather than avoid fearful situations help the client to fight back and believe that they can control the anxiety. This increased self-belief decreases self-doubt and increases self-esteem, thereby facilitating the client to function in a positive circle of self-healing rather than the vicious anxiety trap. Controlling the anxious thoughts, challenging the destructive core beliefs, understanding the causes of their anxiety, and changing their avoidant behaviour, support the client to function with a sense of psychological well-being and help them to feel positive about themselves and their life.

Marina: Change through therapy

Marina believed she was not good enough at anything and therefore really did not like herself. This resulted in her endless concerns about her partner leaving her. She felt she was unworthy of her relationship and that soon he would realise this and leave, which created a sense of impending doom. Marina was constantly plagued by the fear that her relationship was at risk and lived her life in a state of constant agitation. In reality the only factor her partner wanted to change about their relationship was Marina's inability to relax. Marina was selfless in her treatment of her partner because she believed she had to compensate for herself. Every time she put his needs above her own in an attempt to maintain the relationship and compensate for what she considered to be her massive failings, she reinforced her belief that she was simply not good enough.

As with most people struggling with anxiety Marina had an extremely selective perception filter. All evidence that she was worthy would be attributed externally, minimised, or simply ignored. All evidence that she was not good enough was exaggerated, retained completely, and relived over and over again. This selective perception filter was both the cause and maintenance of her anxiety.

In therapy Marina was able to start challenging her belief that she was not good enough. In order to do this she had first to accept that anxiety may be causing her to critique herself with a negative bias. Once we had looked at the psychological effects of anxiety she was able to see that distorted negative self-perception was a common symptom. Once she could accept this theoretically she gained some motivation and trust to begin to look for her negative perception filter. This required a leap of faith that she was not as useless as she believed and that this uselessness was not a 'fact' but a symptom of anxiety. It is truly terrifying for someone with anxiety to begin to hope they may be good enough, because with the expectation of hope comes the risk of profound disappointment that they are truly not good enough and it is not the anxiety making them think those thoughts, but fact. Once someone takes the leap of faith to see the evidence that they are in fact good enough, loved and lovable, it can have a profound effect on them and their life. This idea was completely alien to Marina and in order to start freeing herself from her anxiety trap she needed to consider the possibility she was loved and worthy of love. In order to consider this for a moment she needed to give the idea space. She struggled to do this and needed to take a leap of faith in order to do so. She feared this leap as she realised she could start to hope. Hope felt dangerous as she had previously believed, totally and utterly, that hope would be dashed and therefore even considering the idea meant she could set herself up for heartache, rejection, and pain. To start to believe all was not lost required self-belief and the relinquishing of her view that the impending doom was inevitable.

Over time she questioned her negativity and sense of impending doom, challenged it and recognised it really was not accurate. She came to see that she had evidence she was truly loved and lovable. A sense of being good enough strengthened, began to calm her panic and reverse her relentless negative thinking.

Anxiety in therapy and its impact on the therapist

As a therapist working with anxiety it is easy to apply anxiety-like traits to the therapy itself. Often I can internalise a sense of urgency to help and find that I am trying to increase the pace of progress and plan the sessions too rigorously. This sense of urgency mirrors anxiety sufferers' tendency for manic thinking and rushed ineffectiveness, clearly not what is required of the therapeutic relationship. Calm thinking is required but that reflective peace can feel threatening and even useless when someone needs immediate release from their anxiety. Staying calm and trying to embrace the peace is a challenge in the therapy but is very useful; calm thinking fosters clarity and diminishes the sense of anxiety.

The sense of impending doom that clients describe can sound so rational that several times I have colluded with their concern over the future. I have found myself worrying that my client may truly have a terrible medical problem that is being overlooked or that their work situation is about to implode. At times like this, I have experienced relief on hearing that my client is in the waiting room, ready for their weekly visit, having survived. When this happens it is important to be aware that the anxiety is controlling the therapy and not the other way around.

Anxiety sufferers doubt themselves. It is an important part of our work as therapists to reflect upon our practice and our therapeutic rationale. However, when working with anxiety, our healthy therapeutic reflection can become compromised and result in therapeutic doubt. We can also become trapped in an anxiety spiral so we feel that our work is not good enough and not clinically effective. It can require a leap of faith to sit back and look for the positives in the work and trust that there really are some and not interpret any evidence that we are doing a good enough job as misguided arrogance. This is why clinical supervision is even more important when working with anxiety.

Conclusion

Anxiety is all about losing control (or the fear of doing so) and causes the loss of self-trust and perceived self-control. People avoid situations which they perceive to exacerbate their fears, and can become overly attached to routines which avoid these. The sufferer does not actually lose the capacity for self-control or need to engage in such avoidant strategies, but in certain specific situations they can feel as though they do. This kind of destructive thinking can also apply to smaller and seemingly insignificant decisions. Therefore, the world that the anxious person inhabits is a very hostile place. It's a world full of self-doubt and self-loathing, a world where it seems one has continually to face tests with no hope of passing: success is not an option. Everything is exaggerated and becomes a catastrophe.

People who suffer from anxiety often feel bewildered and confused by the fact that their anxiety is intangible. Therefore, it is important to understand anxiety appropriately. Anxiety can be 'treated' but clients needs help to find their true selves again and defeat the negative filter that distorts their view of themselves and their lives. The therapy needs to go beyond the symptoms and help clients see themselves for who they really are and who they can be; not what the anxiety would have them believe. This requires patience, calm, and the regaining of control over negative thoughts to incite a positive challenge to all critical thoughts and a sense of well-being. The therapist and client need to reach through the fear to find the person behind it, always present, but presently lost.

References

Atcheson, L (2008). *Free Yourself from Fear*. London: Hay House.

Bourne, E (2000). *Anxiety and Phobia Workbook* (3rd ed). New York: New Harbinger Publications.

Bowlby, J (1951). *Maternal Care and Mental Health*. Geneva: World Health Organization.

Bowlby, J (1988). *A Secure Base: Clinical applications of attachment theory*. London: Routledge.

Clarkson, P (1995). *The Therapeutic Relationship*. London: Whurr.

Gelso, C & Carter, JA (1985). The relationship in counselling and psychotherapy: Components, consequences, and theoretical antecedents. *The Counselling Psychologist, 13*(2), 155–43.

Hinshelwood, R (1994). *Clinical Klein*. London: Free Association Books.

Meins, E (1997). *Security of Attachment and the Social Development of Cognition*. East Sussex: Psychology Press.

Padesky, C (1994). Schema change processes in cognitive therapy. *Clinical Psychology and Psychotherapy, 5*, 267–78.

Rogers, CR (1951). *Client-Centered Therapy*. London: Constable.

4

Phobias: Extreme fear in everyday situations

Lucy Atcheson and Martin Milton

Instantly the world changes, I can't breathe, I struggle to catch my breath. I am panting, swallowing hard, my breathing has sped up, and it's almost as fast as my pounding heart. Before I know what has happened I am screaming and I am across the other side of the room, my face is red, I want to cry, I often am crying. If someone doesn't help, if it is still in sight, I lose it. The screaming gets louder, the sweating more profuse and there is no option; I just have to get away. Or else I faint.

As the moment passes, usually because I have left the room or someone has removed the balloon, I am embarrassed. Ashamed even, full of doubt and guilt. How am I supposed to work if I can't control that reaction?

Fear is a common human emotion; phobias are something else, the experience of *extreme* fears. Extreme fear about an object or situation that others might think is an everyday, inoffensive object. We accept that everybody can get nervous, stressed or anxious about something. We all want to move away from an offensive or scary object. It's not simply a conscious or intellectual decision though; it is a powerful embodied reaction too. We see something we don't like, and can be flooded by adrenaline in order to fight it off or to flee. This has been described as an evolutionary response to fear and has come to be termed the 'fight or flight' phenomenon that we will all experience at some point in time.

For some people fear develops into dread and then into terror. Once an object is known to lead to such an extreme sense of fear people want to avoid the object (or anything that reminds them of the object) at all costs. We then avoid even the *possibility* of contact with the object or situation that scares us so much. *This* is a phobia.

Phobias can have extreme and devastating impacts. The promising young city executive can be so terrified of the tube they leave their job because there is no other way of getting there. The confident young mother is so terrified of spiders that she can't go into the room where her baby is because of its presence. The Christmas shopper almost throws themself in front of a bus because they are trying to get away from a mouse in the rubbish bin. Phobias have greater consequences than often imagined. These are not theoretical overdramatic situations; these are actual situations that clients have brought to therapy. In these instances fear comes to dominate lives. Even when not faced with the phobic object people are preoccupied, plotting and planning ways in which they will be able to avoid such occurrences. The phobia comes to dominate all waking thoughts, influence every behaviour and infiltrate every feeling. Basically phobias are common fears, heightened to destructive extremis. A phobia is a complete and utter fear of a specific situation, person, object or animal.

In some ways, phobias are commonplace. Both of the authors have worked with clients struggling with their phobic reactions to different things. The closeness of the phenomenon was brought home again when one of the authors posted that he was writing on this topic on one of the social networking sites. Amongst the pool of friends a number commented briefly about the extent of their own phobias. Nicola said: 'I was at work this morning with a cup of tea in hand and could feel something on my face, the biggest, fattest spider ever!!! (My biggest phobia) and I ended up wearing the tea.' Jacqui said: 'My phobia is Parktown prawns[1] – terrified of the things though I doubt you get many in London … ugh when they stalk towards you it is so scary.' Jacqui went on to comment that phobias occurred more broadly in her family. She said: 'Me – claustropobic, scared of heights, Parktown prawns. My daughter: spiders and Parktown prawns.' And Dipak commented that: 'I can't even look at a cartoon snake without giving a journalist the opportunity to write the immortal words … "before turning the gun on himself". That's how scared I am of those nasty things!'

The focus of a phobia could be almost anything. We hear of people being phobic about flying, crowds and crowded spaces, empty spaces, spiders, balloons, buttons, bananas, snakes – the list goes on and on. Almost

---

1. Large cockroach-like insects that spray at objects they fear and jump when disturbed. Common in South Africa.

anything and everything has the capacity to become the subject of phobias. This is possibly because of the way phobias develop.

How do phobias develop?

Phobias are thought to develop in three main ways. The first way is as a reaction to an actual traumatic experience. It might be that you see a spider and it makes you jump. Unconsciously you put two and two together and you associate being scared with spiders. This assumption is not challenged because you want to avoid them and may be quite successful at doing so. Without, what the cognitive therapists call, normalisation, the spider is never rehabilitated, it never becomes an everyday part of life. If you think about it, it is only to avoid it and the avoidance is helped by ever-increasing 'catastrophic' images, for example of that spider running up your legs or over your face. Because you are avoiding the spider, you build it up in your head that you need to avoid it at all costs, therefore the fear gets worse and you spend your time checking. For example this might develop into a routine where you ask 'Is there a spider in this room?' before you come into it. Before long the fear or dislike or distaste of a spider has developed into a phobia and you can't leave your house because you fear running into a spider.

A second way that phobias are thought to develop is by way of conditioning – when you are very little you see your mother jump into a chair because a mouse runs into the room. It makes sense for that child to conclude that, if my mother is scared of that mouse (and unconsciously the child has assumed that mother is so powerful and knows everything), then mice must be really terrifying. And you copy the fear and that fear develops into a phobia.

The third 'cause' of a phobia is deflection. An example might be that a child is emotionally, physically or sexually abused by a parent whilst it is raining. The situation terrifies them. They are devastated by the situation, but it's so difficult to really acknowledge that it's the parent, the person that's supposed to love them, that is causing them pain, so the pain and the context are conflated and they become fearful of the rain; when it rains it feels like horrible things happen. In this case the child develops a fear of rain because it's even more terrifying to acknowledge that they are really terrified of those that they are reliant on.

These are three common ways in which phobias are thought to develop. People are of course complex and can come to the same experience in a multitude of ways, but these are three very common types of experience which are thought to be instrumental to the development of phobias. Whichever way the phobia develops, the end result is that somebody is completely ruled by their fear of an object, situation, person, animal or food type.

Phobias are considered to be minor concerns by a wide range of people. Clients can feel ashamed about suffering from them and friends and relatives can lack understanding about the experience. However, phobias can have extreme consequences.

Arachnophobia: Real life, not a Hollywood film

Lucy worked with Stella,[2] a client who had a terrifying and restricting phobia of spiders. Her phobia was such that she couldn't walk into a room without scanning and checking for spiders. Leaving the house was extremely difficult because she would expect to see spiders as soon as she left the front door. She was hypersensitive and hypervigilant and it was an achievement to get through the door, let alone to the shops, as this required constant scanning and checking. It wasn't just live spiders that terrified her either; it could be pictures of spiders, a bit of web she saw, even washing on her clothesline that resembled a web. Going to the zoo with her children was impossible because of the creepy-crawly area. Museums or holidays abroad were terrifying for her because of the possibility of a spider's presence.

This phobia didn't just restrict Stella's life, lifestyle and behaviour, it created some very serious family issues and repercussions. When her baby was about eight months old Stella stepped outside into the garden, leaving the baby a few meters away from her in the living room. The baby was close but on the other side of the French windows. As Stella turned to return she realised that there was a spider on the patio. She froze on the spot. This was not just a momentary reaction. Stella was in torment, fearful and frozen, and able to see her baby crying and in distress. Not only could she not reach out to her baby but she couldn't get to her phone to call anyone for assistance. The effect was total; she froze psychologically, emotionally and physically and couldn't move even after the spider had gone, just *in case* the spider came back. After four hours, when the panic did finally ease and she was able to dive back into the house, she was

---

2. In order to protect client confidentiality all identifying features have been changed. Indeed, all case studies here are composites of many clients. The case studies are made up of what constitutes a typical presentation.

exhausted, terrified and filled with guilt and a sense of complete incompetence.

Stella reported this to her GP because she was so worried, embarrassed, ashamed and terrified of her behaviour. Her child ended up on the 'at risk' register because of her fear of spiders. It was at this point that Stella decided to take some action. This is just one example of the way in which phobias don't just make someone scared or uncomfortable, but they can destroy lives too.

People who struggle with phobias are their own harshest critics; they criticise themselves endlessly and relentlessly for having the phobia. The self-criticism is understandable but unhelpful as it exacerbates the feeling of being powerless and incapable; it fundamentally disempowers them, they completely beaten by the phobia and incapable of fighting it. In order to overcome a phobia the person needs to develop and draw on self-belief. If they are endlessly criticising themselves self-esteem can be eroded to such a degree that the person has no reserves on which to draw. Therefore reflecting on themselves differently and recognising their strength and self-esteem is often a fundamental and crucial part of the therapeutic process when working with clients who are phobic.

Working with phobias

A common and useful way to work with phobias is termed 'systematic desensitisation'. This is a process where a programme of deliberate engagement with the feared object or situation is thought about, discussed and gradually engaged with. People sometimes describe this as using a 'graded hierarchy', starting with the least panic-inducing exposure to the object and then gradually working up to much more feared objects/ situations.

A graded hierarchy for spider phobia might look like this.

Stage 1: Spelling the word S.P.I.D.E.R and saying it as a whole

Stage 2: Working with a cartoon of a spider. This might mean looking at it from afar, or holding the picture itself. Talking about reactions and also talking about less panic-fuelled assumptions.

Stage 3: Working with a picture of a spider. As in stage two, this might mean looking at it from afar, and then holding the picture itself.

Talking about reactions and also talking about less panic-fuelled assumptions.

Stage 4: Working with footage of moving spider. The client is encouraged to sit and watch an entire clip directly, rather than from behind their hands or closing their eyes.

Stage 5: Working with a cuddly toy spider. Even though this is a toy spider it can feel 'more real' than a picture or footage as touch is involved. Again, the client and therapist can look at it from afar, and then hold it at arm's length before maybe trying to get close and have it sit on different parts of the body or even be cuddled. Talking about anxious reactions and also talking about less panic-fuelled assumptions.

Stage 6: Working with a dead spider. The process of getting closer is taken an additional step further in this stage as whether it be looking, touching or having the spider on them, the client has moved from the 'idea' of a spider to contact with an actual spider.

Stage 7: Working with a live spider in a jar. At this point avoidance is really being challenged.

Stage 8: Working with a free-roaming spider.

Stage 9: Working with a tarantula skin.

Stage 10: Working with a live tarantula.

The principle of exposure and a graded hierarchy/gradual engagement with the feared object can be adapted to most situations whether they be other feared animals (dogs, birds, mice, etc), objects such as buttons, bananas, syringes and the like, or spaces such as heights.

Often clients find that their phobias actually get worse in the first couple of sessions. This is perhaps because they are talking about them more and therefore they begin to panic about having to face the object they fear. Rather than engaging in each step of the process, clients may become fixated on the final stage in their hierarchy before they are ready. If they are struggling to name their phobia, thinking about Stage 10 can be absolutely overwhelming. Therefore, it's important to remind clients that systematic desensitisation needs to be gradual, cautious and paced but always fully completed. It is important to complete each stage/level of a graded hierarchy before moving onto the next stage so the client gains full benefit, support, and motivation from their success. As previously noted, struggling with a phobia can undermine a person's self-belief in very powerful ways, therefore, if they complete a stage successfully and are encouraged to celebrate this success, their belief in their ability to manage their phobia should increase. This in turn will help combat the next higher-intensity stage. If someone moves up a stage without completion of an earlier stage, their inability to beat the previous stage will manifest in a very critical internal voice that can sabotage managing the task in the next stage of the hierarchy.

Clients need reassurance that when they pass up to the next stage they will feel ready for it. Often it is useful to do some work about limiting thoughts to the present and not thinking too far ahead prior to starting the systematic desensitisation. This is similar to walking down the road and just looking at the next step, not six steps ahead. The process is about encouraging a new, safe engagement with the feared object/situation and not a re-traumatisation.

As with most feared experiences, anticipation is often a key part of the experience, and reality is seldom as bad as imagined. The terror comes from the meaning that the event holds for the person, the expectation that trauma and catastrophe are imminent. As you work through the stages the client begins to realise that they can cope and manage, that they are in fact capable of beating their phobias, or developing the meanings attached to the phobia one step at a time. It can be very empowering for the client to feel a sense of managing their fear as for so long they may have been very critical of their inability to do so.

Phobias and the therapeutic relationship

As mentioned by Joanna Jackson in Chapter 2, there is a lot of empirical work (over a great period of time) to support client accounts that the therapeutic relationship is important across all therapeutic approaches (see Luborsky, Singer and Luborsky, 1975; Rosenzweig, 1936) whether it is behavioural, psychodynamic, existential, systemic, cognitive behavioural or transactional analysis. The therapeutic relationship houses the therapy and enables the client to feel sufficiently secure and safe to do the difficult emotional work that they need to do in order for the therapy to be a success. The therapeutic relationship is especially important with phobias as the work needs to focus on the client's most extreme fear, which is as much physical as it is psychological. In light of this the need to trust the therapist is paramount. How can you face your ultimate fear without the confidence that your therapist is there to support you?

Whether the therapist normally works from a dynamic, systemic, existential or cognitive framework, they have to consider the fact that the nature of phobias means that therapy needs to focus, to some degree, on a behavioural systematic desensitisation, as well as an explanation of the reason why the phobia developed in the first place and how the object came to hold such fear. Therefore therapists need to adopt a more holistic, integrative or pluralistic approach, which can take them out of their preferred model.

The therapy needs to focus on the therapeutic relationship to nurture the client to feel sufficiently relaxed, to really explore their core fears and traumatic memories. This may be easier said than done and there is a balance to be found. Too little challenge and the client may talk a lot but never engage with the phobic experience. Too much challenge and the therapist can feel quite cruel and bullying. Negotiating confidently with the client about degrees of fear is important every step of the way. In light of this, the therapist needs to be fully aware and constantly reflective regarding the impact they are having on the therapy. It can also be said that the client's history of relationships with others needs to be clear in the formulation and needs to be explored when looking at early childhood memories that may have developed into projected phobias. To adopt a style reminiscent of a punishing, scary parent or teacher may not be the end of the world if intellectual development is at the core of change, but deep therapeutic change is a much more holistic process and will not be aided by a compliant reaction based on discomfort, fear or anxiety. Transference-type phenomena often occur when working with the third type of phobia and can be a very useful tool in understanding the true cause of the fear. Often when analysing childhood anxiety that developed into a projected phobia, the client may respond to the therapist as though they were the origin of the fear. This offers information and can create opportunities to enrich the desensitisation work. The therapist needs to be mindful of transference and deal with it so that they do not become overwhelmed by it as this risks silencing the client. Even without complications from previous relationships, the client can refuse to do the desensitisation because of their fear, or because of a protective anger that can occur. Client anger can be difficult to deal with but it is really important to establish whether it is simply a reaction to the fear or a historical artifact. Anger can inform us about the client's way of being in the world, their emotional expectations and how these have come to influence the development of such extreme fears in later life. As mentioned before though, therapy with clients who are phobic cannot really adopt a purist 'either/or' approach. While the therapist should avoid mixing approaches in a chaotic manner, they will need to work in such a way that the same therapy houses both the developmental and behavioural aspects. It is often useful to start with the developmental then take on a gradual desensitisation to the phobic object, which developed because of a projected fear. An example of this type of work is probably best illustrated by a case study.

Rain, rain, go away!

Marc, a gentleman of 33, had a terrifying phobia of the rain. This affected his ability to leave the house because even if it was sunny he was afraid that it might rain later. This fear evolved into a preoccupation with the weather channel, weather pages and the Internet. He developed a terror of winter and would become very depressed over winter months which resulted in a diagnosis of seasonal affective disorder. During his process of therapy we came to suspect that it was more about the fact that he wouldn't go out if there was any perceived likelihood of rain. When caught up in this pattern he became very bored, lonely, stuck in his relationship with nothing but the weather forecast, which resulted in him feeling very low and almost suicidal at times. It is this that finally brought him to therapy.

When Marc presented at therapy and discussed his rain phobia he was in a great deal of distress but the therapy was delayed due to the disabling effect of the phobic situation, his inability to get to the sessions if the weather forecast was not helpful. As you can imagine, a rain phobia is hard to work with in a rain-rich country like the UK.

Once engaged in therapy it became apparent that Marc's entire remembered trauma was related to his childhood. It also became apparent that Marc was resistant to any talk about his father and their relationship. Together, Lucy and Marc developed a tentative hypothesis, that perhaps this phobia with the rain was a projected phobia. This possibility helped facilitate discussion about Marc's childhood and his relationship with his parents, and as he became more at ease he began to disclose a very physically abusive father who humiliated and terrified Marc throughout his childhood. With Lucy's support Marc found the strength to discuss particularly humiliating and physically abusive traumatic memories, all of which involved dark nights and rain. In particular Marc remembered the sound the rain made on the window. It is possible that Marc was focusing on the sound of the rain on the window to try and ignore, or at least survive, the abuse. He may have disassociated himself from the reality of the physical beating he was taking and it became easier to be terrified of the rain than to acknowledge the abusive and traumatic relationship with his father. The phobia really began to solidify when he tried to discuss his abuse with his parents. Both his mother and then also his father completely denied his experience and rejected him. Not only had Marc suffered the traumatic and abusive childhood, he then had to suffer his parents' denial of it as though all the trauma hadn't happened. In the face of such denial and rejection Marc began to really try and deny the experiences and focus more on the fact that he has been terrified of the rain. The phobia had developed and become stronger and stronger as it became incorporated with the rejection of the self and the smothering of the past.

It became apparent to Lucy and Marc that it was important to discuss his relationship with his father and the origin of the fear before any behavioural programme began. Even though this was challenging (as it did not feel like the most immediately supportive approach for his everyday experience), it benefited his therapy in the long term. Marc talked about his relationship with his father and the abuse he had suffered and for the first time in his life it was acknowledged, heard and believed. His trauma was given voice and empathised with and he was supported to show his emotional responses. Furthermore, he started to feel like his fears were rational and made sense in the context of his abusive childhood and the need to dissociate from what was going on. He began to understand his terror of the rain. He made the link for himself that in his childhood he had felt that the rain had somehow caused the trauma, almost as though he could not bear to believe that his father was being so abusive. This allowed him to tackle the desensitisation with greater confidence. In this specific case, the effectiveness of therapy was enhanced by understanding the origin before starting the behavioural desensitisation.

When the behavioural programme began Marc progressed quite speedily through the different stages. His phobic reactions were no longer meaningless, crazy symptoms that came out of nowhere. They were experiences to engage with compassionately and with understanding. Marc 'beat' his phobia of the rain. Moreover, he was able to support himself, even more to like himself and think of himself as a capable fully functioning adult man rather than either mad or bad. The madness in his life had been redirected towards the real origin and not towards himself or any other external object.

Conclusion

While we recognise that this is but just a brief insight into the experience of phobias and ways to work with them, we do hope that readers will find it useful. In particular we hope that readers will recognise that phobias are not unfathomable, meaningless or crazy phenomena – but that they are rich and meaningful, if painful and debilitating, experiences that require calm, respectful understanding. With attention we can go beyond the symptom to important, and sometimes quite profound, understandings.

References

Luborsky, L, Singer, B & Luborsky, L (1975). Comparative studies of psychotherapies: Is it true that 'everyone has won and all must have prizes?' *Archives of General Psychiatry, 32*, 995–1008.

Rosenzweig, S (1936). Some implicit common factors in diverse methods of psychotherapy. *American Journal of Orthopsychiatry, 6*, 412–15.

5

Pain: Working
with meanings

Terry Boucher

An unpleasant sensory and emotional experience associated with
actual or potential tissue damage, or described in terms of such damage.
(International Association for the Study of Pain, 1979)

Hello.

It's eight-thirty in the morning and I've been up a couple of hours sitting
on an uncomfortable chair in a room which I now realise is quite cold. I've
been sitting at my computer trying to think how to start this chapter and
have been looking for something that might be engaging and less formal,
certainly not grandiose or superlative in statement – which earlier drafts
have had elements of being. I have revised what I have typed over a dozen
times and am still 'racking my brains' for something better than 'Hello'.

Am I in pain?

Am I suffering?

In reflecting on these questions it might become obvious that the concepts of 'pain' and 'suffering' have a number of quite expansive dimensions:

Physical: I am clearly physically uncomfortable continuing to sit on this chair in the cold. Particularly the nerves that run from my legs, buttocks and lower back are making me aware of this. This physical sensation that I feel is unpleasant – I feel pain.

Attentional: As my awareness is drawn to the unpleasant sensations in my body they seem to intensify in unpleasantness and I have an urge to move.

Behavioural: I shuffle around in my chair redistributing my weight through changing my posture, I feel some relief but a background discomfort remains.

Environmental (context): The idea of carrying another chair upstairs that might be more comfortable, but which would probably chip the new paintwork in the process causing me more labour in the long run, is not motivational and I'd rather stay put.

Cognitive: I think 'Come on, hurry up, stop getting distracted', 'I've left writing this chapter far too late, I'd better knuckle down and get on with it', and try to focus back on what I'm typing.

Relational: I have a fleeting image of Martin Milton (editor) being very understanding on the phone as I tell him the chapter is going to be late, but visualise him absolutely seething with rage underneath.

Emotional: I'm feeling pretty stuck now and stressed about the progress of this chapter. I'm anxious as to whether the content so far is just a rambling interlude that will eventually be edited out, and thus everything I have typed has been a complete waste of precious time!

This emotional sensation that I feel is unpleasant – I feel pain …

… and I am suffering.

How much am I in pain, and why?

How much am I suffering, and why?

To reflect on these quantifying/qualifying questions, often the first to be asked of any experience, it could be useful to consider a number of factors that might play interrelated roles to lesser or greater degrees in the experience of pain and suffering:

> The *cause* of the pain, whether known or unknown, and the *location* of it.

> The *intensity* and *type* of pain that *is* experienced, or *expectations* of what *will be* experienced.

> The *attributions* that are made about the pain itself; its lived and expected *duration*; the *control* that is had over it; and its actual or envisaged *consequences*.

> One's *previous experience* of pain.

So for me in my cold room the *cause* of my pain is known – the chair, my posture on it, the nerves in my legs, buttocks and lower back (*location*); and ultimately my agreeing to write a chapter, not starting it sooner and thinking there isn't enough time to complete it before the deadline – which leads me to feel stuck, stressed and anxious. The physical *intensity* is relatively mild and I would describe it (*type*) as a dullish throbbing ache. However, emotionally it feels more intense in the moment, quite powerful and while the *expectation* of my physical pain is that it is in my *control* and will be somewhat relieved shortly (*duration*) on physical movement (which I now do and it is, to a degree, relieved), I expect my unpleasant emotions will continue until I have made more headway into the chapter, have a cohesive sense of its content, and ultimately Martin has given me some reassuring feedback – this is not in my control! When I take the time to consider my *previous experience*, not an automatic feat, I do realise that I have indeed been here many times before. I know myself as a bit of a 'catastrophiser', and even if I stopped typing right now and told Martin to find another contributor, ultimately there would be no significantly bad *consequences* for me in my life. When I take the time to do this 'cognitive movement', my emotional pain is also relieved somewhat. I am suffering less.

In many ways what is being suggested through my opening statements – and certainly not for the first time in pain literature – is that the experience of pain and suffering for an individual is likely to be a product of the interplay between a number of dimensions and interrelated factors deeply rooted in the *meanings* of a pain experience for that individual. It is likely to be these meanings, that play out in an individual's pain experience, that dictate aspects of the pain experience itself, as well as its consequent impact on their physical and emotional functioning, and relational ways of their being in the world.

So that is it, the opening of my chapter – pain experience is subjective and determined by the meanings it holds for an individual. 'Pain is what the person says it is, existing when and where the person says it does' (McCaffery & Beebe, 1999).

To illustrate this further it is also important to consider a number of the physiological mechanisms of pain, as per our current understanding, that relate to the elements above and demonstrate the complex interplay between the sensation of pain, the experience of pain, and ultimately the suffering caused by pain.

Conceptualising pain and pain mechanisms: Current models

The first thing to say is that pain sensation is often assumed to be quantitatively linked to tissue state or damage. One might assume that hammering a nail through your thumb will hurt more than banging your elbow on a doorframe. However, there is much evidence to suggest that this simple linear relationship is not actually the case (Moseley, 2007). Think of the pain caused by lemon juice in a paper cut – high pain sensation yet relatively negligible tissue damage. Anecdotal evidence from battlefield surgeons describes incidences of huge physical trauma, e.g. loss of limbs, accompanied by little or no pain experience (Butler & Moseley, 2003). Clearly, pain sensation *in itself* does not provide an accurate measure of the state of tissues/damage.

Given this understanding Gate Control Theory (Melzack & Wall, 1965) was proposed to explain why animals (including humans) show variable response to noxious (nociceptor nerve) stimulation. It put forward that noxious input must be modulated by other non-noxious input within the central nervous system (CNS). It suggested that 'pain gates' – a term used to describe the place where such modulation takes place – are an amalgam of both ascending input, from the periphery, and descending input, from higher brain centres, which impact on the organism's sensation of pain. Over the past 45 years laboratory experimentation has upheld this viewpoint (Meyer et al., 2006) and has demonstrated that pain sensation is modulated by many factors from across somatic, psychological and contextual/social domains (Moseley, 2007).

There has been much research highlighting an evaluative component to pain sensation and how this might subsequently translate into pain experience. Of note *attentional* aspects, of how we focus on pain sensation, have been suggested as important in how we experience it (Eccleston & Crombez, 1999). Our *expectations* of pain (Sawamoto et al., 2000) and the *anxiety* provoked by pain (Klages et al., 2006), whether pain is existent or envisaged, have also been suggested as likely factors influencing how pain is experienced, as well as the *context* in which it is felt (Moseley & Arntz, 2007). However, interestingly the research detail is not clear. For example, some research data suggest that attending to pain and increased anxiety amplifies pain experience while attending away from pain and reduced anxiety reduces it, while other research suggests attention and anxiety might have little impact or quite the opposite effects on pain experience (Moseley, 2007). Consequently, the evaluative component of pain would again seem to be multifactorial and individually subjective with regard to how pain sensation is experienced and what it means to an individual.

The next thing to say, and as Moseley (2007) summarises, the nervous system is dynamic – it changes in response to activity – and any relationship that did exist between the state of the tissues/damage and pain experience weakens as pain persists. Neurons that transmit nociceptive input to the brain become sensitised as pain persists, as do networks of neurones in the brain that evoke pain. This can lead to hyperalgesia, where painful stimuli become even more painful, and allodynia where previously non-painful stimuli now become painful, e.g. sensitivity to touch/movement/heat. As pain persists proprioceptive representation of the painful body part in the primary sensory cortex may change, which may impact on motor control and movement, which in turn can have implications for the pain experience itself (Moseley, 2007). This is often referred to as 'central sensitisation', describing how the whole of the CNS can become sensitised.

As this dynamic process plays out in the nervous system an individual who is experiencing persistent pain is likely to be grappling to make sense of their experience. In this regard pain experience is likely to become the conscious/unconscious correlate of the *perception* of pain/threat (attention); the *meaning* of that threat (beliefs/expectations/anxiety); the *meaning* of pain itself and other somatic output (e.g. swelling); and the *meaning* of pain experience for their social/relational sense of being in the world and in their cultural context.

So again we are back to *meanings*, meanings that will influence the interpretation of pain experience and responses to it, as well as, ultimately its *impact*, and the consequent level of *suffering*. That is, pain experience, its impact, and the suffering felt from it, are *not* necessarily related, rather they are modulated through meanings.

With this said it is also important to bear in mind that pain experience has been closely linked to memory and learning (Apkarian et al., 2009). This has a number of important implications with regard to how we might approach understanding the impact on and suffering of those in pain, particularly if their pain experience has persisted for a long period of time.

Apkarian et al. (2009) suggest that chronic pain can be seen as a state of continuous learning, in which adverse emotional associations are continuously made with incidental events simply due to the persistent presence of pain, e.g. walking, lifting, going out, socialising. Simultaneously, the persistent presence of pain does not allow for extinction of adverse emotional associations which are consequently reinforced. The pain experience can become deeply integrated into memory and experience which establishes at the level of cortical representation and brain circuitry in the limbic system – which plays a role in the experience and 'regulation' of emotions (Apkarian et al., 2009). Thus, the physical and emotional experience of pain becomes deeply enmeshed in cortical structures, and it is further suggested that it is this 'conundrum' of experience, as well as efforts to 'disentangle' the complex associations present, that underlie at least some of the suffering experienced by those with persistent pain.

So the relationship between pain experience, its impact on one's life and the suffering caused by it needs to be recognised as a very complex phenomenon embedded in memories and meanings, and one that is consequently likely to be largely subjective in nature. With this said I will now focus on the nature of 'diagnosis' in the arena of pain.

Diagnosis, chronic pain and counselling psychology

In contemporary Western society human distress and suffering are often explained in terms of pathology and/or psychopathology (origins in the Greek word *pathos* meaning suffering). These explanations are heavily influenced by a disease-focused medical world-view where the alleviation of distress and suffering become the remit of professionals. It is a positivistic epistemological understanding where *objective diagnosis* by a suitably trained professional plays an integral role in quantifying/qualifying another person's experience and guiding treatment interventions; and in this the relationship between 'patient' and 'professional' is dictated in terms of expertise and power (see also Milton et al., 2010). However, there is a potential difficulty with the 'explanatory' assumptions (see also Fletcher and Jackson, this volume) – what if human distress and suffering are not so easily open to *objective diagnosis*?

What if distress and suffering (as suggested above with regard to the experience of pain) are a feature of the complex interplay between an individual's intra-psychic meanings; their interpersonal and relational ways of being in the world *with* those meanings; and the socio-cultural context in which they exist?

Furthermore, what if the trained professional is also at the 'mercy' of the interplay between *their* intra-psychic meanings; *their* interpersonal and relational ways of being in the world *with* those meanings; and the socio-cultural context in which *they* exist – their potential for 'objectivity' consequently called into question?

If these 'what ifs' are entertained then the rather assured unitary criteria of diagnosis become only a small part of a much bigger picture in understanding the experience of distress and suffering; and the expert professional humbled with regard to their own understanding of the experience of another. Put a little stronger – diagnosis as a generalised linguistic descriptor, which by itself says little or nothing about an individual's state of being, is likely to be very problematic if it is used *in itself* to guide attempts at the alleviation of distress and suffering.

In this context it is interesting to consider the nature of pain diagnosis. There is no objective instrumental or procedural test for pain, and practitioners in this field have long recognised the problems with formal medical diagnosis as a comment on an individual's experience. Yet there are multiple diagnostic typologies and sub-typologies frequently used both to describe experience and to convey treatment approaches. The World Health Organization's *International Classification of Diseases – Tenth Revision (ICD-10)* (World Health Organization, 1997) recognises that pain is likely to be co-morbidly present in a number of 'conditions', for example:

Chapter XIII: Diseases of the musculoskeletal system and connective tissue (M00-M99)
    Dorsopathies (M40-M54)
      Dorsalgia (M54)
        Low back pain (M54.5)

Here 'low back pain' is a sub-sub-sub category of 'diseases of the musculoskeletal system and connective tissue', and used as a descriptor of specific pain location and nothing else. More widespread pain conditions are also categorised in this chapter of *ICD-10* (e.g. Fibromyalgia (M79.7).

In *ICD-10* if pain is not referable to any one tissue, organ or specified body region it is categorised in:

> Chapter XVIII: Symptoms, signs and abnormal clinical and laboratory
> findings, not elsewhere classified (R00-R99)
>> General symptoms and signs (R50-R69)
>>> Pain, not elsewhere classified (R52)
>>>> Acute pain (R52.0)
>>>> Chronic intractable pain (R52.1)
>>>> Other chronic pain (R52.2)
>>>> Pain, unspecified (R52.9)

Here it can be seen that sub-sub-sub-category diagnoses have a temporal aspect with acute pain distinguished from persistent pain or chronic pain. Chronic intractable pain (R52.1), sometimes referred to as 'chronic pain syndrome', is often diagnosed after time has been allowed for any healing processes to complete. While there are diagnostic disparities as to the length of this time period, Turk and Okifuji (2001) pragmatically suggest that chronic pain should simply be seen as 'pain that extends beyond the expected period of healing'. A benefit of this suggestion is that it can be employed to cover a range of experiences and allows for the factoring out of any other explanatory factors for the persistence of pain, such as complications in tissue healing or the presence of other conditions that might be expected to cause pain, such as rheumatoid arthritis.

It has been estimated that around 19 per cent of the European population experience chronic pain in some form (Breivik et al., 2006). Chronic pain is often divided into two categorical distinctions: 'nociceptive pain' – indicating nociceptor nerve activation either 'superficial', e.g. on touch of the skin, or 'deep', e.g. on movement of muscles or within organs (Coda & Bonica, 2001); and 'neuropathic pain' – indicating the presence of nerve damage or malfunction, either 'peripheral' or 'central' depending on location within the peripheral or central nervous system (Bogduk & Merskey, 1994).

Given the diagnostic outlines above it will be apparent that such categorisations of pain in themselves say little or nothing about an individual's pain experience, its impact on their lives, or the suffering encountered – if indeed someone with pain is suffering. For this, as already stated, it is apparent that we need to consider meanings – and it is at this level that counselling psychologists, and other reflective pluralistic practitioners, are likely to be particularly adept at working.

A counselling psychology approach, with its inquisitive, pluralistic and open-minded attitude to how we come to 'understand' experience, would seem particularly relevant in working with an individual's pain experience. That is, the subjective intra-psychic meanings of their pain; their interpersonal and relational ways of being in the world *with* those meanings; and the socio-cultural context in which they exist with pain. Counselling psychology's resistance to theoretical dogma and simplistic or reductionist 'pathologising' diagnostic medical understandings of experience, *in themselves* as an adequate comment on experience, give it a broader stance from which to approach phenomena like pain. Its continual questioning of its own assumptions sees it attempt to gain a richer perspective on what it is to be human in relation to experience, distress and suffering. In this spirit, counselling psychologists take a relational stance to the phenomenon itself, challenging trends and traditional ways of seeing the 'individual' as a self-contained entity, pointing to the relational ways of humans *being* with each other, both in their internal and their external states (see also Manafi, 2010). In this counselling psychologists cease to be experts on the experience of another, rather they aim to become a shared partner in the exploration of such experiences, and in this exploration it is recognised that both are changed.

In what follows I will attempt to convey aspects of this ethos or 'spirit' of counselling psychology as an approach that steps outside of diagnosis in a human-to-human encounter. It is my sense that by attempting to narrate such aspects it might be possible to draw out the qualities of approaches that go '*beyond diagnosis*' and consequently their relevance to helping others.

Working *with* those *with* pain?

Acute or short-term pain is something we are all likely to experience everyday. It is part of our physical/emotional attributes that generally serves us well in identifying and avoiding dangers. It is a fast teacher – when a child puts their hand in a flame they quickly learn not to do it again. Those that are born with inhibited or absent nociceptor action are prone to significant injuries and shorter life expectancy.

Working as a psychologist in the field of pain one has to be cognisant as to the positive attributes of pain. However, when pain shifts from an acute time-frame to a more chronic or long-term experience there can be a number of 'impacts' on a person's 'biopsychosocial' functioning (Turk, 1996) and consequently their suffering. It is usually in these instances, where pain has been diagnosed, that physicians are unable to alleviate it pharmacologically or through direct intervention, and where suffering is identified, that psychologists come to work with those who experience pain (see Hession, 2010 for an outline of aspects of psychological work in a pain context). If someone is in pain but *not* suffering they are not likely to be referred to a psychologist or pain services.

While at this point I could go into a whole host of psychological models – including psychodynamic, cognitive behavioural, and acceptance-based conceptualisations of pain, with their differential evidence bases – outlining the advantages and disadvantages of differing delivery formats – from individual to group based, in the 'treatment' of chronic pain, I'd rather not, I'd rather talk about my experience of Barbara and of myself in the role of psychologist!

Referral

Barbara, whose name and identifiable information I have changed as necessary to protect confidentiality, was referred to a chronic pain service in which I work with a diagnosis of 'chronic low back pain' and a recommendation for 'pain management strategies'.

Looking at the referral letter and demographic detail I know Barbara is a woman in her early 50s. I know her address, her GP's details and that she does not smoke. I know she experiences pain and that this is likely to be localised at least in part in her lower back. I know that following a scan showing herniation of two discs in her lumbar spine surgical intervention has not worked for her, she has also been diagnosed with 'failed back surgery syndrome' (Long, 1991). I also know that various pharmacological approaches have proven of little benefit. I know that serious life threatening co-morbidities ('Red Flags'), that could account for her pain experience, have been ruled out by physicians – it is 'benign pain'. I know she has experienced pain for 17 years with gradual onset, worsening ten years ago on the birth of her third and last child, and worsening yet further following her 'failed' surgery six years ago. I know nothing about what her pain means to her, the impact it has on her life, or her suffering. This is a common referral – from my perspective not much to go on, but possibly from the referrer's, enough. It is my job to find out more – 'to assess'.

I work in the NHS. I have 45 minutes allocated to 'assess' referred clients, and place them on one of four pathways:

Pathway 1: Suitable for and likely to benefit from group pain management programme, waiting time approximately three months.

Pathway 2: Not suitable for group pain management programme but likely to benefit from pain management strategies – individual work indicated, waiting time approximately seven months.

Pathway 3: Not suitable for pain service at current time – refer on and inform referrer.

Pathway 4: Not suitable for pain service at current time and requires no referral on or does not wish to take up service – inform referrer.

Barbara's 'assessment'

After introductions and while I am still outlining the nature and purpose of 'our meeting today' (preferred to 'the assessment' identifying me as 'assessor') Barbara acknowledges she is well versed in repeating the details of her pain experience and unprompted proceeds quite light-heartedly in describing her history of pain chronologically. She outlines its location, 'lower back, left leg sciatic nerve and sometimes right leg' and her beliefs as to its initial cause, 'general wear and tear'; and escalation – child birth in her forties – 'at that age you're not so geared up for it'. She categorises the different medical interventions and rates their impact on the type and intensity of her pain. She shows little emotion in describing her surgery and the worsening of her pain thereafter. I take notes and listen. It all seems quite simple, matter-of-fact and I am relieved – I have another three assessments this morning.

In the spirit of the narrative so far I ask quite matter-of-factly about how Barbara's pain impacts on her life. I am caught off guard by the sudden change in presentation. There is silence, I watch as Barbara goes red, looks away and starts to cry. I think along the lines 'you idiot, you've totally misjudged this', and take time to manage my own 'catastrophisations' about my clumsy matter-of-fact question. I reflect that the well-versed light-hearted narrative is a defence against more powerful and disturbing emotions that accompany Barbara's pain, and that I was more than happy to buy into her well-versed narrative to attain some relief from the service pressure I feel I am under.

In what follows Barbara identifies that her back pain impacts on her ability to walk distance, sit for duration, and play with her children, aged 10, 13 and 15 years – they are sporty as she once was, but now she watches as 'other mums' play sports with them. In the moment I catch myself thinking back to my own childhood growing with a loving mother diagnosed with multiple sclerosis – and particularly one sports day where she motivated herself to run in the parents' race. She fell and people laughed not knowing her condition and how it would make her feel, it was her last sports day, she didn't come again – I am crying inside with Barbara in the room, after all I laughed as well. Barbara tells me she has not been sexually intimate with her husband for at least five years due to the pain and her fear that intercourse would make things worse. She thinks her husband is hiding his frustration with this and she feels guilty. She says she is letting her family down, is a burden to them and they would be better off without her – she is crying outside with me in the room. I resonate profoundly with Barbara's tears and in my 'humanness' want to hold her tight, love her in her sorrow and make things better. I want to help. I'm also 'a professional'. I am experienced in 'bracketing off' my-*self* from the *other*. I must get on with my job, the next assessment is due to start in 15 minutes and I feel a contrast of emotions at this thought – sadness, frustration, fear, anger, stress.

As I continue to explore with Barbara the impact of her pain experience, now more a person-to-person experience, its meaning becomes apparent. For Barbara her pain *means* she is restricted in a number of deeply valued physical activities, which in turn *means* she can't be a good mother or wife, like 'other mums'. It *means* she is letting her family down, is a burden to them and they would be better off without her.

Imagine that … feeling as if you are letting your family down (those that you love most), are a burden to them, that they would be better off without you (if you were gone – dead!). I'd feel pretty shitty. I'd feel pretty selfish and would probably try my damnest to minimise my 'failings'.

Barbara reported that she 'coped' with her pain by 'putting on a brave face' and 'not letting others in' to see her suffering – as I noted 'Barbara acknowledges she is well versed in repeating the details of her pain experience and proceeds quite light-heartedly in describing chronologically her history of pain' – she is skilled in descriptions of experience that can defend against acknowledging their impact and meaning. She is skilled in protecting others, including professionals, from the horror of who she feels she is – a burden, a failure.

[In writing this I ponder how diagnoses as descriptions can allow professionals to defend against acknowledging the *lived* impact and meanings of experience, and relationally having to 'empathise' with them – after all empathising can be painful.]

Barbara reports that she tries to push through her pain and not show it to her family. She says she pretends all is fine and described how she does as much as she can on 'good pain days' while on other days is in so much pain that she's 'on my back and useless'. She avoids sexual intercourse fearing penetration by her husband will increase her pain, rationalising that it escalated after childbirth and thus could be related to her 'woman's parts'. She reports she was hopeful the surgery would fix things and the pain would go, instead it got worse; she blames no one but herself and wishes she hadn't agreed to the surgery – 'a stupid mistake' – she wants no more surgery though it has been mentioned by one of her consultants.

According to service protocol for any assessment I assess Barbara's risk to herself and/or others. She reports that while she can at times feel she is letting her family down, is a burden to them, and that they would be better off without her, she would not act to hurt herself in any way saying she knew at some level this would 'only damage them further' – she feels stuck and hopes our service can help.

[As I reflect now I consider how my clumsy matter-of-fact question about the impact of the pain on Barbara's life caught her off guard in her well-versed narrative – exposed her to less familiar and comfortable 'realisations' of her situation, and consequently left her more exposed to the raw emotional meanings of her pain for her and her family. In the room I learnt about her suffering, re-lived some of my own suffering, and it felt to me that we had a very human contact. 'Clumsy interventions' have value.]

At the end of the assessment I discuss with Barbara the service options and I suggest that the residential four-week group pain management programme might be beneficial. My rationale being in part that it had the shortest waiting time and that being with others who experience pain may help Barbara contextualise some of her own pain experiences. Furthermore, I suggest its week-day residential nature might also allow her some 'respite' from the feelings of guilt she experiences when she is with her family (though it was acknowledged she might feel guilty leaving them), which might allow her to focus more on developing strategies to reduce the impact her pain has on her life, and her level of suffering. She said she had read the service literature and understood that 'pain management' in its focus is not about reducing pain levels in themselves but rather about learning coping skills.

Helping Barbara: 'Treatment'

Barbara attended her four-week residential pain management programme. During this time she works both individually and in group with a multidisciplinary team of physiotherapists, occupational therapists, clinical nurse specialists, and psychologists. I was Barbara's contact person as I had 'assessed' her and we met several times to discuss her experiences on the programme. At the end of the programme we met once more to reflect on the programme, its impact, and the future for Barbara. The following titles try to encompass some of the themes of Barbara's reflections.

Understanding pain

Barbara reflects that while she was initially sceptical of the chronic pain message, based on the literature (e.g. Moseley, 2007) that chronic pain is not necessarily linked with ongoing tissue damage, through gradual grading up of physical activities over the four weeks and gaining confidence in such activities she felt less stressed/distressed by her experience of pain. It no longer means she could not do things, rather she could do them but would experience pain. She says 'I experience pain if I do them or don't, so I might as well do them and sod it.' She says that on the last weekend home she had spent more time with her children playing catch in the back garden and for her this was wonderful, 'I feel like a mum again'. I feel joy with her in the room, smile and praise her.

'I hate pacing – but I do it anyway'

During the programme it was suggested to Barbara that the way she approached tasks and activities seemed to fall into an 'activity-rest' cycle which could be fueling her pain experience. She acknowledged she tended to push through pain and 'overdo' on better pain days, suffering for days after 'on my back'. Though she reflects it went against her 'instincts', during the programme she practised breaking activities up according to time/

duration or number/quota, 'I don't do all the ironing now – three shirts and that's it for the day', and increasing such times/quotas gradually – 'pacing-up'. She reported that she hated having to do this but recognised that she tended to have more even pain days with fewer flare-ups, 'so there must be something in it'. I'm cognisant that we all probably have to do things in ways we don't really like doing them, and note that I hear what seems to be acceptance in Barbara's tone as she talks.

Talking about pain

Barbara tells me she talks to her family more readily about her pain rather than 'putting on a brave face'. She says not hiding it seemed to make her less stressed and she notes, 'it's hard, bloody hard at times, but if they know then at least they can understand'. At this point Barbara stutters over her words and I can see tears well in her eyes. On exploration her tears seem to mark the importance of understanding – being understood by others, not feeling one has to convey a 'false-self', to be 'real' – she says, 'I feel closer to them if I can talk to them, not like a defective train holding them back'. It seems in her tears that she is less worried about protecting me also, is able to tolerate that she will impact on others and in this again I sense a person-to-person contact, I am deeply moved at this sharing but resist the urge to share back my own tears which I hold inside – I generally don't allow myself to do this as a person, not just as a 'professional', sometimes I wish I did.

In her tears Barbara smiles and says she has talked to her husband about sex and '*pacing this up*' – we both laugh seeming to enjoy the lighter interlude in the acknowledgement of pain management 'catch-phrases'. She says that she now recognised that her 'fear-avoidance' (Vlaeyen & Linton, 2000) of sexual intimacy with her husband was something that made her feel incomplete in her relationship, guilty and lowered her self-esteem. She says, 'I'll spare you the details but things are much better.' I smile and say 'thanks'; we both laugh navigating this 'socio-cultural' awkward moment.

Barbara's future

Barbara says she feels much more hopeful about her future. She reflects that the psychology-focused sessions in the programme helped her realise how she relates to herself, 'I spend lot of my time beating myself up when it's not my fault'. As a consequence she says she can catch herself doing it – 'It's like a habit' – and reports she is more able to dismiss such thoughts thinking to herself how well she has generally managed for so long – her children are doing well at school and are 'good kids'. She also says she is less critical of herself regarding her back surgery, something we had reflected on in one of our meetings earlier in the programme, saying resignedly 'it was worth a try'.

Barbara says she has planned a holiday for her and her family – camping in the New Forest – which was something she had done in her teens. She says she is both daunted and excited by the prospect, but glad to be even considering such a venture, previously believing she would probably be housebound before long.

Terry's reflection

From my perspective it seems that Barbara's pain has changed in meaning. It no longer *means* she is restricted in a number of deeply valued physical activities, which in turn *meant* she can't be a good mother or wife, like 'other mums'. It no longer *means* she is letting her family down, is a burden to them and they would be better off without her. It seems that as these meanings have changed so has her 'stuckness' – she is moving both physically and psychologically – and ultimately she is suffering less, and *I have* helped. Joy – my sense of self and professional esteem remain intact and I am proud – I like occupying the role of a psychologist at such times, after all it allows me such experiences.

[I note to myself that such 'happy endings' of helping another is what largely reinforces me in my work as a psychologist, but that there are many types of ending experience. It is ultimately the uncertainty of such experience in which I find I have some agency that allows me to define some sense of who I am – that is my motivation.]

References

Apkarian, AV, Baliki, MN & Geha, PY (2009). Towards a theory of chronic pain. *Progress in Neurobiology, 87,* 81–97.

Bogduk, N & Merskey, H (1994). *Classification of Chronic Pain: Descriptions of chronic pain syndromes and definitions of pain terms* (2nd ed). Seattle: IASP Press.

Breivik, H, Collett, B, Ventafridda, V, Cohen, R & Gallacher, D (2006). Survey of chronic pain in Europe: Prevalence, impact on daily life, and treatment. *European Journal of Pain, 10*(4), 287–333.

Butler, D & Moseley, GL (2003). *Explain Pain.* Adelaide: NOI Group Publishing.

Coda, BA & Bonica, JJ (2001). General considerations of acute pain. In D Loeser & JJ Bonica (Eds) *Bonica's Management of Pain* (3rd ed). Philadelphia: Lippincott Williams & Wilkins.

Eccleston, C & Crombez, G (1999). Pain demands attention: A cognitive–affective model of the interruptive function of pain. *Psychological Bulletin, 125,* 356–66.

Hession, N (2010). The counselling psychologist working in a pain context. In M Milton (Ed) *Therapy and Beyond: Counselling psychology contributions to therapeutic and social issues.* Chichester: Wiley-Blackwell.

International Association for the Study of Pain (IASP) (1979). Pain terms: A list of definitions and notes on usage. *Pain, 6,* 249–52.

Klages, U, Kianifard, S, Ulusoy, O & Wehrbein, H (2006). Anxiety sensitivity as a predictor of pain in patients undergoing restorative dental procedures. *Community Dental Oral Epidemiology, 34,* 139–45.

Long, DM (1991). Failed back surgery syndrome. *Neurosurgery Clinical North America, 2*(4), 899–919.

Manafi, E (2010). Existential–phenomenological contributions to counselling psychology's relational framework. In M Milton (Ed) *Therapy and Beyond: Counselling psychology contributions to therapeutic and social issues.* Chichester: Wiley-Blackwell.

McCaffery, M & Beebe, A (1999). *Pain: Clinical manual for nursing practice* (2nd edn). St Louis, MO: Mosby.

Melzack, R & Wall, PD (1965). Pain mechanisms: A new theory. *Science, 150,* 971–9.

Meyer, R, Ringkamp, M, Campbell, JN & Raja, SN (2006). Peripheral mechanisms of cutaneous nociception. In SB McMahon & M Koltzenburg (eds) *Textbook of Pain* (5th ed). London: Elsevier.

Milton, M, Craven, M & Coyle, A (2010). Understanding human distress: Moving beyond the concept of 'psychopathology'. In M Milton (Ed) *Therapy and Beyond: Counselling psychology contributions to therapeutic and social issues.* Chichester: Wiley-Blackwell.

Moseley, GL (2007). Reconceptualising pain according to modern pain science. *Physical Therapy Reviews, 12,* 169–78.

Moseley, GL & Arntz, A (2007). The context of a noxious stimulus affects the pain it evokes. *Pain, 133,* 64–71.

Sawamoto, N, Honda, M, Okada, T, Hanakawa, T, Kanda, M, Fukuyama, H, et al. (2000). Expectation of pain enhances responses to nonpainful somatosensory stimulation in the anterior cingulated cortex and parietal operculum/posterior insula: An event-related functional magnetic resonance imaging study. *Journal of Neuroscience, 20,* 7438–45.

Turk, DC (1996). Biopsychosocial perspective on chronic pain. In RJ Gatchel & DC Turk (Eds) *Psychological Approaches to Pain Management: A practitioner's handbook.* London: Guilford Press.

Turk, DC & Okifuji, A (2001). Pain terms and taxonomies. In D Loeser, SH Butler, JJ

Chapman & DC Turk (Eds) *Bonica's Management of Pain* (3rd ed). New York: Lippincott Williams & Wilkins.

Vlaeyen, JWS & Linton, SJ (2000). Fear-avoidance and its consequences in chronic musculoskeletal pain: A state of the art. *Pain, 85,* 317–32.

World Health Organization (1997). *International Statistical Classification of Diseases and Related Health Problems* (10th rev). Retrieved 21 May 2011 from http://apps.who.int/classifications/apps/icd/icd10online/

6

Relational Trauma:
The boy who lost his shadow

Louise Brorstrom

This chapter focuses on relational trauma by way of caregiver misattunement. It will explore how shaming experiences are a form of misattunement that rupture a child's, and later the adult's, ability to form and maintain intimate and trusting relationships with self and others, and the way it leaves the person with a difficulty regulating their emotions. This chapter focuses particularly on the hidden shame that could create narcissistic defences that may or may not lead to a diagnosis of a personality disorder. It looks at shame as a 'relational trauma' that is not explained within a diagnostic framework such as the American Psychiatric Association's *Diagnostic and Statistical Manual of Mental Disorders (DSM-IV)* (1994) or the World Health Organization's *International Statistical Classification of Diseases and Related Health Problems (ICD-10)* (1992), but can have considerable debilitating consequences for the individual. I will explore this trauma by briefly discussing misattunement and shame, and then look at the content of several sessions with one of my clients, who I will call Nathan, and I then discuss the implications for therapeutic practice. All patient names are pseudonyms and steps have been taken to ensure Nathan's confidentiality. Nathan has also given consent for me to use our work in this chapter.

Misattunement: Creation of the shadow

Relational trauma can be experienced when the caregiver is consistently misattuned to the child's emotional experience. This can be through emotional/sexual/physical abuse, but can also be related to experiences that might not legally be categorised as 'abuse'. These experiences may sometimes be classed as 'less severe' but are still marked by the inability to respond appropriately and sensitively to a child's emotional experience. For example, if a child says 'I'm sad' and the caregiver responds 'No you are not,' the child's experience is negated, invalidated and/or dismissed and the child concludes that 'I must be wrong about how I feel' or 'I'm not OK'. At the time, it may not *seem* important, but when misattunements are frequent they can create a rupture of the self–self and self–other relationships. Over time this creates the sense that somehow there are parts of the child's self that are unacceptable and should be negated, invalidated and/or dismissed as they are felt to be a threat to the child–caregiver relationship. The child fears rejection and abandonment if s/he continues to feel that which is unacceptable. These aspects of the self become a threat to the social bond which the child needs to survive in the world. As a survival mechanism the child starts a splitting-off process where parts of itself are shed, cut off or hidden. As one of my clients said, 'I feel like I have to hide behind a mask, because if someone really sees me it is excruciating. I can't stand it. It is like I was disconnected from my soul and I have lost half of me.'

Siegal (2010) writes that our neural pathways are, in large parts, dedicated to tuning in to the internal state of the other. He argues that attunement creates the platform for development of the self and for secure attachments between the infant and the parents. We are essentially unable to establish secure attachments if we are not attuned with ourselves. He also explains that it is through attunement with another that we are able to take in another's internal world and let it impact us. Gerhardt (2004) explains that if the caregiver cannot accept the child's full range of emotions, the child will struggle to be accepting and interested in her/himself. She goes on to argue that misattunement leads to feelings being felt as ambiguous bodily sensations, either unpleasant or pleasant, but without processing and understanding. Schore (2003) suggests that, with the absence of an attuned caregiver, the child remains emotionally overwhelmed and as a result s/he is unable to develop emotionally. Consistent misattuned responses may leave the child unable to know what s/he is feeling and, thus, incapable of expressing it.

Relational trauma caused by misattunement is hidden within the dynamic of the relationship. It is hidden because neither the child nor the caregiver is in a position to notice or work with these ruptures. For the child, it is how the world works and they have little choice but to accept what relationships are offered. It is possible that, for the caregiver, the ruptures in the relationship with the child are unconscious and often due to his/her own unresolved relational trauma. It may be that the caregiver is well meaning and caring, but is, for whatever reason, unable to fully connect with the child. These ruptures damage the child's, later the adult's, ability to be present in relationships with self and other and lead to a sense of shame. Lansky (1999) noted that shame serves a purpose; he notes it is an emotional regulation system that ensures that social bonds are maintained. The system is complex because each individual experience varies greatly, but it signals that one's survival in society/family is threatened, by, for example reduced social standing, lovability, acceptability or possible immediate rejection. For a child, this could be devastating as abandonment could mean death, being as they are, so utterly dependent on the adult for physical and psychological survival. Thus, it could even be suggested that the shaming experiences function to ensure compliance with the system, whether it be the family system or greater society. Schore (2003) says that the shame blocks arousal that regulates excited states like mania, excitement and euphoria. This is similar to Kohut's (1971) idea that shame is a way of terminating interest in something when one is in a state of excitement. Shame does eventually limit or even block self-exploration and curiosity as this has become a risky and possibly dangerous thing to do. It chains the child to the ground, communicating that it can be risky and threatening to explore.

Nathan: The lost shadow

Nathan came to me when he was suffering from severe depression and several attempted suicides. He was an artist in his late thirties, but when he walked in the room he seemed about 17 years old. He felt life to be grim and dark. There was something about him that reminded me of Peter Pan, that magical flying boy who does not touch ground and who does not want to grow old. One remembers Peter Pan with a naivety and a smile, but if one looks closer it is a rather dark story about an angry, desperate and controlling boy who is lonely and does not belong anywhere. Like Peter Pan, there were times when Nathan would 'stay flying' and never touch ground, finding it hard to rest. During these times Nathan would come to therapy with tales of adventures, some pleasant, some violent. J.M. Barrie (2009) notes that Peter Pan would have dazzling stories about his daily adventures, but one was never quite sure what was true and what was not. I had a similar experience with Nathan.

When Nathan came to therapy he was in a pit of depression. It seemed he had come crashing to the ground and felt unable to fly. He explained that he was brought up in a family that was caring overall. However, it soon emerged that he experienced frequent and consistent misattunement when it came to feelings and expressing more aggressive and, perhaps, masculine parts of himself. He said,

I grew up with my four sisters and my mum. My dad was not really around much. I was looked after, cared for. I mean, I had five women looking after me. I think I was looked after so much that, in such a sweet way you know, even when I would get angry I would get sweetness, if that makes sense. I remember that it would get me so angry because I felt ridiculed for feeling angry.

Nathan's mother was perhaps well intended. She probably wanted to nurture him and make him feel OK and she may have had difficulties with knowing how to manage aggressive emotions. The absence of an attuned father may have made it even more difficult, for both mother and Nathan, to manage and communicate these emotions. Nevertheless, Nathan's experience of this misattunement was that somehow his potency and aggression were unacceptable, 'I felt ashamed, it was so humiliating'. Shame communicates that there are areas that should be hidden, not shown to anyone else. The threat to Nathan was that if he was to express how he really felt, his mother might not know how to handle it and he could face rejection from the caregiving relationship. Aggression was rejected and replaced by sweetness. To remain loveable and acceptable he began a process of shutting down these more aggressive parts of himself, which meant that Nathan did not learn how to notice, tolerate, regulate or express these types of emotions. When he experienced anger it was fused with feelings that it is shameful to feel this way. It became important to ensure that these types of feelings were tucked away in the dark shadows, never to be seen again. In essence, the process of hiding parts of himself had ruptured his ability to fully know himself, as well as his ability to be present in relationships with others.

Seduction

As a consequence of finding parts of himself threatening Nathan developed a defence against these feelings, one that stopped them leaking out, one where he appeared sweet and pleasant. This manifested in therapy, as the following passage shows.

N: I think I am lucky getting therapy, being able to talk to such an intelligent and pretty woman like you. I usually find it easier to talk to women and most ...

I interrupted him at this point as it felt a very loaded, quite powerful moment and one he did not seem to be aware of.

L: Hold on. I feel I need to stop you there. I am noticing that I am blushing and feeling embarrassed and that makes me wonder what is happening. Are you flirting with me?

N: Ahm ... I ... [silence for a few seconds] ... I guess I was really.

L: I think we need to explore what that is about for you.

N: Ahm ... I think that is what I do. I do that with women. I am used to flirting with women. To make them like me ... My sister was always pretty dominating. I remember, and this happened many times, when she used to get angry with me and she would yell and shout. I remember being about three or four and it really continued throughout our whole lives. I never knew how to defend myself against her so, what I used to do was to just be so sweet and agree with her, because I knew that would make her even more pissed off. So when she started arguing with me I would just agree. She would get so angry and I loved it.

L: So there are times you feel dominated by women, your sister, me and your way to feel more in control is to quietly dominate, because that comment felt sharp.

N: Hmm. Did it? Oh, I am sorry. I didn't ... Well I guess you are those things that I think I am not. You have done your degree, doctor ... together ... have it sorted. I am just a loser artist that can't do my art, I have no money, can't stand up for myself and oh I don't know. Shit.

L: It makes you feel like less of a man.

N: Yes ... [silence].

Seduction had become one way for Nathan to express his potency without having to take responsibility for it. To me, this moment in therapy mirrored how Peter Pan flew into Wendy's room to charm and dazzle her, to convince her to come to Neverland where he could be in control. However, Nathan came to therapy, like Peter Pan came to the Darling house, to find his shadow, the parts that he had lost so long ago. His relational impetus was to reconnect with those lost shadow parts, but looking into the shadow can be terrifying and frustrating, and instead he tried to seduce me. In this process I felt remnants of shame, humiliation and degradation. It was as if he had given me his shadow. It was as if a foreign object had invaded and penetrated me. In absolute terror to be seen, he seemed to be undermining his own therapy. This is reminiscent of Peter Pan instilling fear in the lost boys so that they would do exactly what he wanted. Peter Pan had even been known to threaten to kill to get his own way. Just like that, Nathan was prepared to 'kill' me with seductive attacks to make sure I did not come too close. His shame was projected into me in the sessions, because there was no way he ever wanted to experience such shamed potency again, but it was not working. Rather than dancing in the sunshine, the therapeutic relationship had his shadow placed right in the middle of it. We could both see it, but could we bear it?

Helpless depression

In the following sessions Nathan mainly expressed helplessness and hopelessness about himself and that his life would never be any different from what it is. The seductive boy had transformed into a needy baby that wanted to be fed and rescued from the shadows.

> *N: I don't know if I will ever get better. I just seem to always do this to myself ... I am such a loser. When I am at home I just keep thinking that I might as well just kill myself and I imagine ways of doing it, but ... then I want to be alive, but I can't even do my art, I don't have a relationship, I seem to get tired all the time ...*

> *L: That's a dilemma. We have got quite a bit of time and I wonder if it might be helpful to explore this further by using something called two chairs. I will explain it to you and you can tell me if it is something you want to do ...*

At this point I provided an explanation of the technique in light of our formulation about different aspects of himself that were in conflict.

> *N: Sure OK. So when I am here I am the more vulnerable part then?*

> *L: [Nods]. Can you give me a sense of this part of you?*

> *N: I feel small, like a boy. I might be about 10 or 11. I guess I am about this high. It's me really when I was a kid. I am pathetic. Scared.*

> *L: What would the 10-year-old you want to say to the other part of you that seems critical and self-defeating?*

> *N: I want to have a life.*

At this point a lot happens non-verbally. Nathan shrinks into the chair and seems to fade away. He looks down and seems to find it difficult to look at the other chair. His voice gets lower and it is hard to hear what he says. There is a silence of a couple of minutes.

> N: Oh I don't know. I guess, please leave me alone [he glances up at the other chair]. I just want to be able to do what I want to do without you constantly hounding me ...

Seeing that he had expressed frequently suppressed feelings and aspirations I intervened.

> L: Do you feel ready to get into the other chair? [N: nods] Can you describe this part of you?

> N: Oh how weird. I feel so powerful in this chair. Like, taller. There are two of me here. One part is like a Skinhead that just wants to kick the shit out of that little kid. You know wearing the Skinhead clothes, shaved head, boots ... And then the other man who is like an academic looking down at me from the top of his glasses. Humiliating me. That one is more powerful.

> L: OK. It sounds pretty powerful. What do you want to say to this other part of you?

> N: You fucking loser. You will be nothing. You are a stupid piece of shit that will never achieve anything. You want to have a life? I don't fucking think so. You think you are an artist? You are completely useless and nobody really thinks that you are any good ...

This is just a section, Nathan talks at length and his voice is powerful and loud. Once he had made his point powerfully and the emotion had been expressed I intervened again.

> L: That's what you are doing to yourself every day. Come back to the other chair. What do you want to say back?

> N: [He changes chairs and sits in silence.] Nothing. He is right ... OK. Leave me alone! You have no right to treat me this way [Nathan is growing in his chair, his voice is getting louder.] I am just as intelligent as you are and I can do whatever I want to do, I am so sick of you hounding me. SHUT UP!

We spend some time exploring this internal conflict that is constantly pounding him into a depression and rendering him immobile. When the end of the session is coming Nathan says:

> N: When I came in today I think I wanted you to take care of me, like my mum or my ex-wife always used to do.
>
> L: To take these difficult feelings away.
>
> N: Yes.
>
> L: It's time though, we will have to end for today.
>
> N: OK ... [He sits at the end of his chair and is hesitant to go. He looks up at me.] Well, that's great. What the fuck do I do now then? [He storms out the door.]

Endings are as meaningful as any other part of therapy. This was a powerful moment and helped me realise that if he cannot seduce me, maybe he can call on my maternal instincts to pick him up and tell him that it will all be OK. This is, after all, the experience he has had in his early life. When feelings were strong and difficult he got reassured and nurtured, and of course wanted these things. Yet, underneath this vulnerability he was experiencing rage and fury at his needy parts, at his persecutory parts and at me for not doing what he wanted me to do. In the shadow lies his potency that is so excruciating to feel. Helplessness had become another way of Nathan defending against the shadow parts. However, what he also lost along the way was his potency, responsibility, individuation and the possibility of change.

Subdued rage

From then on, Nathan started to fly. He did not want to grow up and have to be responsible for his feelings and actions. Perhaps he did not know how to. The needy baby was transforming again, into something quite different. He was changing into an angry, provocative and unpredictable adolescent on a perilous journey. He started showing up in therapy attempting to seduce me into his care-free and provocative world. I was beginning to feel that if I did not fly with him in his care-free world, he would leave me or even destroy me for continuing to show him his shadow.

L: You seem a bit different today, and I smell wine. Have you had a drink today?

N: Hmm. No. Well yeah maybe. I met this woman yesterday and we spent the day together, drinking and having sex all night [he looks up at me sharply when he says this.] I might have had a drink this morning. Just some wine ...

I felt stabbed straight in the chest and I started to feel dizzy and unable to think. As if he had killed me off. Again, here were these so familiar shadow feelings of deep shame and humiliation. It was too painful for him to allow me to see those feelings in him. He wanted to hide and in an attempt to get away he catapulted his shadow into me.

L: What just happened in here now? I got a sense of some powerful feelings. And I think we need to understand it. What was going on for you now?

N: [silence] I guess I hated that you asked me if I had had a drink. I thought fuck you! ... You know I was thinking about this one time when I was maybe 12 or 13 and I had left school early and I went home to sit in the shed. I sat there for hours and I remember thinking, I could get away with anything. Do anything I want.

L: You sound furious.

N: [nods] I am. I think I am going manic again.

It seemed that being able to bring the shadow back into our relationship and let him know that I still saw it and that it needed to be explored allowed him to land just for a moment. Later something remarkable happened. He showed some willingness to take responsibility for his flight. He was starting to think about how to ground himself in times of great anxiety, to stay with these powerful feelings. Was Nathan beginning to reattach his shadow?

Murderous attacks

In the therapeutic relationship Nathan had attempted to meet me with seduction, attacks and helplessness, to ensure that I would not see the hidden parts of him and be another woman to shame his potency. To protect himself from reliving the rupture in his early caregiver relationships he shut down any exploration of his internal world through the use of defences. While this protected his internal world, it led to tremendous fury. When seduction or helplessness worked it would give rise to fury because he felt that he 'had' to act like this to be in a relationship. He had to deny aspects of himself. Conversely, he also felt fury when these defences did not work because then he felt under threat. Initially he had tried to manage these conflicting feeling with alcohol, but like for most of us, alcohol made him less inhibited. It seemed to fuel his rage.

In one of our sessions, Nathan came in retelling how he had been bumped by a car and how he had had to restrain himself from attacking the man in the car who seemed ignorant of the damage he had done. Nathan described how he carried some of his work tools in his pocket and how he could have done 'damage' to this man if he wanted to. He explained:

> N: I always carry a Swiss army knife.

Nathan looks at me in a challenging manner and reaches in to his pocket to pull out his Swiss army knife. He does not open it, but sits with it in his hand.

> N: ... See I could have done real damage.
>
> L: That feels threatening to me.
>
> N: ... I guess that I feel pretty dangerous. Here you take it ...

Nathan puts it down on the table between us.

> N: That way you don't have to be scared of me.
>
> L: [I look at it unsure of what to do.] You want me to take it? I think it is better you put it away in your pocket.

He looks disappointed at this and puts the knife back in his pocket.

> L: What do you think you are trying to tell me?
>
> N: That I'm really pissed off and I don't know what to do with it. I'm scared.

For Nathan to acknowledge so clearly how he was feeling was a step forward. I experienced fear and great uncertainly in this session. I felt unsafe and threatened by him but unsure as to how to handle it. I could only imagine how powerfully Nathan was experiencing fear and threat in the session with me. He wanted me to know or to experience the full wrath of his internal world that he continuously experiences. The more his façade was slipping the more desperately he was trying to defend.

I explained to Nathan that I would not feel comfortable seeing him if he carried a knife. So for the next session he put his knife in his bag and we left the bag in the reception. Perhaps responding in this way to Nathan communicated to him that I was taking him seriously. I was not treating his potency with sweetness, but rather I acknowledged the felt threat. This allowed for genuine exploration of what was happening in the relationship and how threatening he found it to be in a relationship that did not respond to his defences in the way he was used to. He talked about how he used to harm himself in the past by trying to create air bubbles in his bloodstream and for the first time he really explored his suicide attempts. He said that he had come to realise that these were ways of him expressing his rage in a way that did not harm anyone else. He revealed that he had attempted his suicides in his mother's house so that she would find him. He was able to think about how furious he was with her and explained that sometimes when he talks to her he has violent images of what he could do to her. For a moment the shadow was out and explored. He has said that since that day he no longer carries a knife.

End of therapy: Reattaching the shadow

Therapy had allowed for Nathan's defences to appear in the room and to shape him. First, it was the seductive boy that flew in and wanted me to come away to Neverland with him. Then it was the helpless baby that was seeking rescue and comfort. He then appeared as an angry and provocative adolescent and finally, the violent and forceful man. Each of these seemed to have served Nathan well in the past. They had been necessary defences to protect him against experiencing excruciating shame. However, he had come to therapy to find those darker parts of himself and to reintegrate this shadow. At this point in therapy it seemed he was moving closer to a helpful position where he could begin to integrate some of his shadow parts.

One of the propositions in the beginning of this chapter was that with the absence of an attuned care-giving relationship, the child, and later the adult, does not learn to regulate emotions. In Nathan's case his early experiences had not helped him learn to regulate powerful emotions such as potency and aggression. He would become overwhelmed when these emotions arose. These 'messy' emotions were driving his life powerfully, yet they remained hidden in the shadows. Unfortunately, when these emotions were discarded, so were responsibility and individuation.

Therapy allowed Nathan to explore the different corners of his shadow. He experienced that which he felt unpleasant, but also rediscovered his own potency and individuality. Jung (1981) wrote that individuation is a matter of a maturation process of one's personality. In the beginning of this chapter I wrote that when a child is misattuned with, it leaves him/her unable to continue maturing. Rather, the child's, and later the adult's, development of emotions remains delayed. Therapy must then work for an attuned relationship so that the client is given the space to restart the halted maturation process. Nathan's maturation process as a person and, in particular, as a man, had been halted. However, with an attuned reparative relationship he had been able to begin individuating. Nathan expressed that 'I'm starting to feel like I know what it is like to be a man. A man I want to be.'

Nathan's progress in therapy, I feel, was mostly due to his own willingness to enter into this perilous journey with me. Although he found it painful, he stuck with it and attended. More than that, he allowed me to impact his internal world. It was as if every stitch applied to reattach his shadow was excruciating, but he was longing to feel whole and remained in therapy. Of course, this will be an ongoing journey, but he has started on the journey to discover himself.

Implications for practice: The relationship

Reflecting on the title of this book 'Diagnosis and Beyond' it seems that in this instance the traditional medical diagnostic criteria could be considered misleading and unhelpful for Nathan. A diagnosis of, for example, severe depression, narcissistic personality disorder, borderline personality disorder or even bi-polar disorder, would not tell us anything about the origin of Nathan's difficulties, nor would it reflect the meaning making around his struggles. I would even suggest that a diagnosis can shut down exploration around suffering and certainly would miss early relational trauma. It becomes a barrier to unpacking the client's experience and, thus, halting maturation and reparation.

Towards the end of therapy Nathan and I explored what therapy had been like for him and what it was about the therapy that had been helpful. He explained that he had found therapy excruciating, painful and life changing. He felt that having had a safe space to explore the darker side of him had been central to his change process. When I asked him what safe meant for him, he said that he had been able to express all of him and that

I had really seen him. 'I think I tried to hide in therapy, but you would not let me. I hated it, but I know it was what I needed.' It seems that having had the experience of being in an attuned relationship had been reparative for Nathan.

As mentioned earlier, attunement is the ability to take in the internal world of the other and allow it to shape one in the moment. It is not a one-way process, rather as in this case it is two people affecting each other. To start with, my main task was to allow Nathan to impact me so that I could attune to him in a way that he needed. In Nathan's case, his early experiences of expressing potency and aggression had been intertwined with shame that eventually shut down these aspects of him. The therapy was about letting these powerful feelings emerge. These had to be experienced by Nathan in the therapy, but also by me. I had to allow his internal world to affect me, then respond in a way that communicated openness, acceptance, as well as boundaries. After all, attunement should not be confused with 'everything goes'. It *was not* acceptable to bring a knife into therapy, but it *was* acceptable to feel powerful feelings of rage and fear.

This way of working puts the therapeutic relationship at the heart of therapy. It is essential for the therapist to be able to form attuned relationships with clients. The relationship needs to allow the early relational ruptures to emerge in the here and now, so that they can be explored. That is of course easier said than done and requires considerable effort and insight on the part of the therapist. It is important for the therapist to be open and self-reflective. Essentially, the therapist needs to be able to be fully present in the relationship and able to reflect on when s/he is not. Siegal (2010) forcefully makes the point that as therapists we need to unshackle ourselves from our own personal chains to be able to attune with others. How could we possibly begin to be present with another if we are preoccupied or blinded by ourselves? In working with Nathan it became imperative for me to explore and understand my own experiences of shame, domination, rage and the erotic.

Letting a client affect us in this way can be a frightening thing to do. To be present with someone, not knowing what will emerge, makes both client and therapist feel vulnerable. One is not hard pressed to see why practitioners, including myself, may want to avoid this. I know that I have certainly wanted to hide away from meeting a client with presence and openness, as a way of protecting myself. I often find this is because I may be overwhelmed by a client, distracted by something in my personal life, feeling unsupported or it may be that what the client brings up touches on something unprocessed in my life. It may feel easier to create a barrier between me and the client. This is why the care of the therapist is important: self-care and professional support and supervision of the therapist is fundamental when working this way and if that attuned support is not there I doubt a therapist would be able to maintain presence and openness without being overwhelmed and possibly burning out. Of course it is down to each therapist to find ways of becoming present and connecting with themselves and to know what their needs are. There are many ways in which this can be done – some may choose personal therapy and/or mindfulness practices, but like Nathan, we all have to find our own way. The metaphor of Peter Pan helped me realise that we would do well to learn from Wendy. With the assured support of the people around her, Wendy had a sense of calm and purpose with which she was able to empathise with Peter but also show him boundaried mirroring. Like Wendy, we need courage to withstand the confusion, seduction and aggression of the other in a way that is attuned, unshaming and productive.

References

American Psychiatric Association (1994). *Diagnostic and Statistical Manual of Mental Disorders* (4th ed). Washington, DC: American Psychiatric Association.

Barrie, JM (2009). *Peter Pan and Wendy*. Dorking: Templar Publishing.

Gerhardt, S (2004). *Why Love Matters: How affection shapes a baby's brain*. Hove & New York: Routledge.

Jung, CG (1981). The archetypes and the collective unconscious. *Collected Works of CG Jung* Vol 9 Part 1. Princeton, NJ: Princeton University Press.

Kohut, HC (1971). *The Analysis of the Self*. New York: International University Press.

Lansky, MR (1999). Shame and the idea of a central affect. *Psychoanalytic Inquiry, 19*, 347–61.

Schore, A (2003). *Affect Regulation and the Repair of the Self*. New York: Norton.

Siegal, D (2010). *The Mindful Therapist: A clinician's guide to mindsight and neural integration*. New York: Norton.

World Health Organization (1992). *International Statistical Classification of Diseases and Related Health Problems* (10th rev). Geneva: World Health Organization.

7

Borderline Personality Disorder: Ending with diagnosis

Tim Knowlson

I knew more than anything that I wanted them to remember. I wanted to go on living in someone's memory. If we are not remembered, we are more than dead, for it is as if we had never lived. (Maitland, 2008: 457)

Introduction

This chapter has two key foci. The first is to try and understand the phenomenon of what is called 'borderline personality disorder'. The second is to consider the specific impact of endings within this phenomenon. Therefore the chapter starts with a definition of borderline personality disorder drawing on psychiatric diagnostic frameworks and also considers some of the wider issues associated with this. The chapter will then move on to discuss therapeutic experiences. I take a personal stance in relation to all of these different areas.

So what do we mean when we talk about borderline personality disorder? The American Psychiatric Association's *Diagnostic and Statistical Manual of Mental Disorders (DSM-IV)* describes borderline personality disorder as 'a pervasive pattern of instability of interpersonal relationships, self-image, and affects' (APA, 1994: 654). There are nine *DSM-IV* criteria, of which five must be present to diagnose this often misunderstood character style. People with this diagnosis can present with frantic efforts to avoid real or imagined abandonment and may show a pattern of unstable and intense relationships, often alternating rapidly between idealisation and devaluation. Furthermore, an unstable sense of self can be evident, the affective instability due to a marked reactivity of mood and chronic feelings of emptiness. Other hallmarks of the diagnosis can include impulsivity in two areas of potentially self-damaging behaviours and recurrent suicidal behaviour. According to the diagnostic criteria, people can also present with inappropriate anger and transient stress-related paranoid ideation, delusions or severe dissociative symptoms.

Over the years, I have worked with many patients presenting with many different issues and concerns. One patient group that has made particular impact on me are my patients with this diagnosis of borderline personality disorder. Working with patients with this diagnosis can be extremely challenging, not only because of the characteristics outlined in the *DSM*, but in part, because of the sense of chaos, confusion, impingement and surprise they can elicit in you. Working with these patients often confused me, frightened me, inspired me, shocked me, annoyed me, impressed me – they each really impacted on me and I'm still processing the impact of working with them today.

One common theme occurred though. In many therapy sessions a key theme of struggling to establish and maintain a therapeutic relationship developed between us. Sometimes this came through direct attacks at me and my role in the room. I was experienced as either too much or too little, too demanding or too absent. With other patients I was kept pushed away by less attacking ways, for example some patients would skip from topic to topic or struggle when I brought our relationship into the frame. Although establishing and maintaining a therapeutic relationship had been effortful, I have often felt alive in the sessions with patients who have tested me and my boundaries. It has been very difficult for both parties to see and hear each other, but we have got there, understanding each other, hating each other, and loving each other. My patients have sometimes appeared to me like a prickly hedgehog baby that desperately wants to be held and nurtured, but as the experience is painful, they seem to be passed around from person to person suffering a lack of containment in the process – and that affects the therapeutic process too.

During therapy sessions I have attempted to contain my patients in a good enough way, and in the sessions I have, metaphorically, 'fed the baby milk'. This symbolism is inspired from the writing of Winnicott (2007). By 'milk' I mean words, thoughts, time, space, control, privacy, power – all a piece of self. In talking therapies – as therapists and patients – we give the gift of words to each other which are little pieces of our thoughts, beliefs, and emotions; we feed parts of our own interpretive self to the other in order to help the patient develop and grow. In therapy something is given and something is taken both by therapist and patient based on conscious and unconscious dynamics (Casement, 1985). Sometimes the baby refuses milk, and sometimes spits out the milk, and sometimes suckles endlessly – and slowly something new comes to the horizon just when the relationship is safe enough. Something that needs to be worked with and through. Both patient and therapist look up from the reverie. An ending happens.

I invite you to join me in my thoughts and ideas as I reflect on the endings of several therapeutic encounters and what the ending could have meant for our therapeutic relationship. I need to ask what endings mean for me and my practice? This work offers space to think and play with potential meanings for me and for the client. Some meanings can be found in the research and theoretical literature and I have often found that theory can be grounding, helpful in generating perspectives in a world of not knowing and confusion in the therapeutic endeavour. And yet, at the same time, I feel theory, jargon and diagnosis comes at a price; we can lose the patient's experience as well as our own. Interpreting and describing can often turn to proscribing rather than staying and being with. Theory and jargon create a language that can, and does, impinge on the intuitive language that can be generated spontaneously and organically between therapist and patient. So in part, this chapter is a way that we can play with the theory, ideas and feelings I have about this experience. As mentioned previously, this chapter is written from the first-person perspective, as it is important to convey the personal sense of working with these experiences. I want this to be an engaging experience for you. I have used my own clinical experience, my own personal views and theoretical research. I know there is a risk in this approach – the question of 'Will I be understood?' is just one! Immediately I feel I need to clarify that as I speak in symbolic terms of mother/father and child, I don't mean to infantilise the patient or remove their potency; it is way of speaking of the reparative and nurturing from past family experiences and in the here-and-now relationship between therapist and patient.

It is also important to note that any patient details have been masked and pseudonyms have been used to protect identities.

Two sections follow. The first moves us on to the concept of borderline personality disorder with regards to the perception of abandonment; the second section looks at ways of working when the threat of abandonment manifests in relation to the ending of therapy.

The 'phallacy' of a borderline diagnosis: Why women?

A critical and curious stance is important when we consider the diagnosis of borderline personality disorder. If one wasn't critical or curious, then this phenomenon would not have been researched or theories disseminated regarding it. A critical stance highlights a potential bias in the diagnosis. Clinical experience suggests that women are more likely to receive a borderline personality disorder or histrionic personality disorder diagnosis than men. Men are more likely to be diagnosed with antisocial personality disorder or dissocial personality disorder. This impression is supported by research. A meta-analysis by Widiger and Trull (1993) highlighted that 75 per cent of those diagnosed with borderline personality disorder were female. Maier et al. (1992) also found higher prevalence rates among women. Having said this, the picture is not completely clear as other studies contradict this, some studies finding no gender prevalence differences (Lenzenweger et al., 2007), and other studies report higher prevalence rates for males (Coid et al., 2006). In a community study by Torgersen et al. (2001), it was found that men experience higher rates of diagnosis of personality disorders including antisocial personality disorder, whereas women did not have higher rates of any personality disorder (including borderline personality disorder). We shall consider three areas in which a bias in diagnosis can occur. Firstly we shall consider patient gender bias, then we shall turn to clinician gender bias and finally we will explore the impact of clinician theoretical orientation on the diagnosis.

Patient gender bias

There is currently much disagreement in the literature. Becker and Lamb (1994) argue that a small but significant size of diagnosis in their study was based on the gender of the patient, a bias of a stereotypical and gender-laden value. Becker and Lamb found evidence that if patients were female, a bias towards a diagnosis of borderline personality disorder rather than post-traumatic stress disorder (PTSD) with similar patient presentations of trauma was found. According to Wallston and Grady, female behaviour has often been explained by personal and intra-psychic elements rather than environmental or external elements. They write 'gender has been used as an explanatory variable, although it is frequently confounded with situational factors such as status and power' (1985: 10). In other words, a woman's gender is used to make a diagnosis rather than considering what has happened to her. Gender bias has been found in psychiatric texts with women being severely under-represented in psychiatric examples and vignettes, except where conditions are associated highly with women (Leo & Cartagena, 1999). Garb (1995) refutes gender bias in the making of a borderline personality disorder diagnosis as inconsistent, unreplicable and an over-exaggeration of results by Becker and Lamb. Garb (1997) reported that when exploring race bias, social class bias and gender bias in making clinical judgements, a bias was mostly limited in nature or not present at all for the majority of clinical tasks carried out, especially in the diagnosis of borderline personality disorder. On the other hand, Garb does mention that a replicated gender bias was found for men who are more likely to receive a diagnosis of antisocial personality disorder and for women who are more likely to receive a diagnosis of histrionic personality disorder. The bias he reported showed that women were predicted to be less violent (but actually were more violent than men). Other researchers argue that what we are seeing are true gender differences (and gender similarities) being brought to light in borderline personality disorder assessment (De Moor et al., 2009; Johnson et al., 2003). Hartung and Widiger (1998) explain differences in gender prevalences as the results of common sources of error such as biases in sampling and biases within the diagnostic criteria.

Therapist gender bias

In terms of the gender of the clinician, Becker and Lamb (1994) found that female clinicians tended to diagnose PTSD for both male and female patients, more than male clinicians, where some gender bias was found for male clinicians who gave females the diagnosis of borderline personality disorder more frequently. Other studies report no clinician gender differences in diagnosis (Ford & Widiger, 1989; Woodward et al., 2009).

Therapist modality bias

Interestingly, a third bias has been discovered in the research, that of clinician modality. It is suggested that a clinical presentation will be diagnosed differently depending on theoretical training and background (Linehan, 1993). Psychodynamic clinicians have been found to diagnose borderline personality disorder more frequently than other clinicians and CBT clinicians have been found to diagnose similar presentations as PTSD rather than borderline personality disorder (Morey & Ochoa, 1989; Woodward et al., 2009). According to Woodward et al. (2009), there is confusion for some clinicians in distinguishing between borderline personality disorder and PTSD trauma.

Regardless of this inconsistent view, the overarching empirical evidence supports the fact that more women are diagnosed with borderline personality disorder. Further disagreement exists in the literature as to why this is the case. Quite clearly diagnosis is made in a relationship by the giver and receiver and so biases and gender misattributions may be occurring in this process. Are women still perceived in Western psychiatry and psychology as 'more emotional' than men, resource dependent on men for security and hence respond to feared abandonment and imagined rejection with emotional strategies? Are men then seen as responding to fearful emotional events by aggression instead? Unfortunately there is not enough space to consider this pertinent topic further, but it is important to recognise that the label of borderline personality disorder may be a sexist stereotype remnant or something that captures a true gender axiom. Certainly with the ambiguity of the vague and catch-all borderline diagnostic criteria, the role of power and gender are at work in the room as clinicians and patients come to grips with the diagnosis. On this note we need to turn to the issue of the therapeutic relationship.

Issues for the therapeutic relationship

The therapeutic relationship – as any relationship – can be endowed with the issue of biases in perceptions influenced by power and power imbalances (Gottlieb et al., 2009; Spinelli, 2006). Diagnosis and therapy can only work when there is collaboration between patient and therapist. The therapist must always be aware of the power imbalance and how this could potentially play out in the room. According to Proctor 'there is a danger that in challenging the "realism" of patient's thoughts that material realities of power are ignored and deemed "unrealistic"' (2003: 14). Furthermore, Proctor writes, 'to refer to compliance rather than "collaboration" would be more honest and accurate and explicit about the nature of power relations involved' (ibid: 15). Some argue that collaboration mostly occurs when the patient has taken on the therapist's world-view, and the word collaboration insinuates equality which may be an impossible task with the inherent power dynamics in therapy (Foucault, 1980; Lowe, 1999). So a critical and curious stance is necessary when *working with* diagnosis as much as when we think about it.

The meaning of endings

the way that, deep inside the misery
    of daily life,
        love lies bleeding.
(Hoagland, 2003: 16)

Diagnosis is not a destination, it is not an end. It is a means to an end. Diagnosis is not just a label on a letter or a patient note; I see diagnosis as a signpost to greater understanding. But it is just that, a signpost, a benchmark of the journey yet to be carried out. And like any signpost on a journey it can be followed or a detour can be taken. In my practice I choose to look at the diagnostic signpost and consider it with the patient, and how they make meaning from it. I have been shocked and dismayed over the years by how such labels have been given from upon high without explanation or without making it personal for the patient. Working with the presentation in the frame of therapy is where the process comes alive, and where the journey can commence for both therapist and patient. In this section I want to focus on abandonment, one of the key diagnostic criteria. In my experience, abandonment has been a central theme to the work; in particular it has been at times of endings when I felt most loved and hated by patients. Some patients didn't seem to experience the approaching ending as independence, aloneness, or even isolation, but abandonment. The patient felt abandoned, and I felt abandoning. Rejected and rejecting, crushed and demanding. There was a sense of negative action on my part. And now that I am in a reflective space which is impingement free, with time to think and feel, I see that I readily interpreted the ending of the therapy as a system and service limitation – and it may be that my own defence against separation anxiety and loss were also at play. My patients perceived it as someone whom they have become attached to letting go before they were ready to walk. Endings have meanings that may – or may not – be shared but they need to be explored.

Making meanings with clients

Breaks and abandonment

Endings need preparation with all patients, but especially with patients who have been diagnosed with borderline personality disorder due to this enhanced fear of abandonment and inner emptiness. Winnicott writes of being weaned from breastfeeding, and I liken that to the ending process of therapy. The therapist has to risk the hatred, fear and frustration of the patient as well as the love and appreciation if a full integration is to be achieved. Winnicott (1991) writes:

> But the breast-feeding experience carried through and terminated successfully is a good basis for life. It provides rich dreams, and makes people able to take risks. But all good things must come to an end, as the saying is. It is part of the good thing that it ends. (p. 81)

In some ways holidays can be thought of as good dress rehearsals of eventual endings and temporary absences can be used to prepare for this. Holiday breaks test separation–individuation in the relationship between therapist and patient. This process is akin to when the infant differentiates out of the symbiotic union with the mother and develops a separate identity. The infant tests his/her own boundaries and boundaries in the relationships with others and the world around. Separation–individuation process is the differentiation between self and other, the maturing of the ego and receiving self and other object constancy. There is a two-fold process of separation where the mother is perceived as a separate self and where the infant goes for a greater testing of autonomy and self-control. Many psychodynamic thinkers believe the separation–individuation process is disturbed in patients with borderline personality disorder (Fleming, 1975).

Opal

I remember working with a middle-aged woman I shall call Opal. Opal presented me with an 'out-of-sight, out-of-mind' like quality. Either I was there in front of her, or gone and dead. There was a need for constant reassurance to feel connected to the other, when the other was gone, so was the transitory sense of self, which the other provided. Holidays proved to be very difficult for Opal and for me. Upon my return she was rejecting, angry, frightened, worried, isolated, self-contained, and leaking out. I often felt guilty, confused and like we were back at square one. It seemed that with mirroring, the mirror had gone, and so had anything stable. In the build-up to a Christmas break Opal would ask more probing questions about what I would be doing during the vacation (I reflected that maybe she was curious if I would think of her), she would skip from topic to topic, closing off from the break, yet revealing painful childhood memories and open new areas for exploration as if keeping me interested till the end. In the build-up to the Christmas break I would use immediacy to explore how she was feeling about our relationship in relation to the imminent holidays. After Christmas I asked her what it was like not having me there, and she responded that I had left her and she was scared of ending therapy. She recalled very painful childhood memories of being left alone as a child and so we linked the past, the therapeutic relationship and present relationships together. We explored how she would feel as therapy would end. I celebrated with her that although she missed me, I was not destroyed and we both survived; I reminded her of her robustness. Together, we considered other ways of remaining empowered during other breaks and resources she could use. What would she do with her time? What could she do differently? What other sources of support were important to foster?

By the Easter holiday she was able to do things with her partner, be more active, and I became a little less important, but not dead. She somehow seemed more able to deal with imminent separation and I experienced some relief. And yet when the end of therapy arrived, our relationship was, in Opal's eyes, terminated and destroyed. I asked her, 'You mention that this is the end, and in some ways it is, but can you imagine me thinking of our work together, me wondering what you are doing during this time in the future.' She replied, 'No.' I had other patients, I was busy, she hoped she mattered – but she couldn't entertain me thinking of her. I gently challenged her, and said that she had made a big impact on me, and that I would not forget her. Our work was ending, but it would live on within us.

A theory that has really helped me in understanding transferential and counter-transferential feelings in therapy when working with abandonment is mentalisation theory (Fonagy et al., 2007). This theory describes how a child's ability to mentalise (understanding others' feelings, understanding others' intentions, the understanding of rules and conventions, and understanding that others have minds) is vital in knowing about self and other. Fonagy (1989) writes:

> The absence of parental figures endowed with adequate empathy to react appropriately to the child's growing social awareness may contribute to a permanent impairment of structuralisation leading to the child's poor comprehension of his own and others' mental states. (p. 107)

The ability to mentalise is considered vital for autonomy and functioning relationships (Fonagy, 1993). People with a borderline personality disorder diagnosis can feel empty because they lack a cohesive sense of self and feel that others have no mind (Fonagy, 2000). I wanted Opal to realise that I came back from holidays, and when the end occurred she would keep existing within my mind as I could in hers – a process of object constancy. This is the ability to pull up internal representations in one's mind when the mother or caregiver is absent, with the ability to self-soothe. According to Auerbach and Blatt (1996) object constancy is severely disrupted in patients with borderline personality disorder. With this ability disrupted, it can lead to the borderline individual being unable to alleviate the panic and terror which comes from the threat of separation, and being vulnerable to the experience of empty aloneness, resignation, and despair (Richman & Sokolove, 1992).

In therapy I tried to give Opal a different experience of ending, an ending that was thought about, that was prepared for. This ending did not come from nowhere. Opal said to me in one session that this ending was not like her other endings which were painful, shocking, and sudden. I was a man who did not just leave her without warning. I was not the father who died abruptly or partner who encouraged her to trust and open up, abused her and then left her. This was a prepared and predictable ending with some sense of newly found control for her. The umbilical cord was stretched and tested before it was cut.

Chris: Gifts in mind

Chris was a young father I saw while still in training. He struggled in a relationship with his wife and he felt unable to open up to her, yet angry and frustrated by not being helped. In Chris' eyes, people just didn't want to help. To me, it felt like things were never enough. Chris struggled to open up to me and commented on my age, training status, and my assumed childless existence. How could I possibly know what it was like for him? A fair point, but it was so attackingly presented. As the end of therapy came nearer, Chris stated that he felt he had wasted time, by not taking advantage of the process. Yet he started to cancel sessions and to berate his own participation in therapy. Towards our final session he warned me that he didn't want to come to therapy. I reflected to him that in the past it may have been easier to reject someone or something before they do what he fears most, which is reject and leave him. Our work had been to celebrate Chris' new ability to ask for help, to endure waiting for possible imperfect help and ensure in the referral process that the appropriate help was sought. I encouraged him to stay with the ending with me and I explored with Chris whether help could be good enough and what would happen if he felt dependent on the help. What was the fear like to want something, to get it and then have it end or taken away. I attempted to reinforce that although he had only started with therapy, work was being done, it wasn't all or nothing, it was something.

After I said goodbye to Chris at our last session, I went downstairs. I found a book in my pigeon hole. It was wrapped in plain white paper. He had written no name and left the book with the receptionist. The book was both anonymous and yet familiar, as I had seen him reading it in the waiting room and we spoke about it once in our session. Although the book was namelessly given, I knew who it was from. He had tried to connect with me through the book that we had once talked about. But the book was given after we had finished and not during the last session. I felt pleased that we had co-created something of meaning for him and the book was given as a thank you. But the timing also struck me as odd. It was like I was kept outside until the very end, when vulnerability, fear and risk were minimised by showing those aspects right at the end. The book was curiously tantalising of what could have been. Perhaps the book was something bad or unfinished in the relationship. The book symbolised something of 'remember me'. Remember the point being explored in this chapter is that people who have been diagnosed with borderline personality disorder more readily feel abandoned because they have a transient sense of self and other; they lack object constancy and due to their limited ability to mentalise cannot hold the thoughts of self and others in mind (Dazzi, 1998). Chris perhaps couldn't imagine me thinking of him. That he would live on in my memory and I would live on in his. I wonder if he couldn't comprehend having 'another human being having your mind in mind' (Weinberg, 2006: 252).

I also came to think about the book in a different way. Winnicott (2005) wrote about transitional objects and transitional phenomena, the first-not-me objects (outside of the child) linked to a transitional space, between the inner world and external reality, a space of play, fantasy and creativity. The transitional object is often linked to the comfort of a mother, for example, but is separate from her also. It can reassure against the anxiety of separation. According to Winnicott the transitional space lies 'between the oral eroticism and true object relationship, between primary creative activity and projection of what has already been introjected' (2005: 2–3). The transitional object allows the child a sense of illusion and control over the world, especially with the relationship with the mother. It helps facilitate fantasy and play. And if the illusion of control is sensitively attuned to by the good-enough mother, the gradual disillusionment encourages the child to need the transitional object less and less while adapting to the environment (Winnicott, 1959). In such circumstances the fusion between inner and external reality runs smoothly and continues to allow for a transitional space in adulthood. Could the book have been a sign of independence on Chris' part? I wonder if I was, for a time, the good-enough mother and father who encouraged some nurture and repair, and my 'son', gaining some self-awareness and independence, left home. He gave me his objects back. I was left holding something for him that may have not been needed. I wish I could have explored the gift with him, and the intimacy and play it could have meant for him.

Conclusion

Don't think it was all hate
That grew there; love grew there, too,
Climbing by small tendrils where
The warmth fell from the eyes' blue

Flame. ...

(R.S. Thomas, from 'The Cry' in Astley, 2002: 129)

Human beings are social animals that enjoy and need to be alone. For some, aloneness is met with relief, peace, space to think and feel, sacredness, and sense of control. Yet at other times, and for others, aloneness is met with fear, isolation, loneliness and feelings of abandonment. The difference between these different ways of reacting is how we are with and within ourselves. Our ways of relating to others is synonymous with our relationship with our own sense of self, our own sense of space and our own sense of boundary. A solitary life seems to me to be one where solitude needs purpose, meaning, ritual, and self-acceptance. People with a diagnosis of borderline personality disorder seem to be engaged in a continual social paradox of desiring to merge with someone, having fear of being alone, fear of being unloved and yet fearing being overwhelmed, of being hurt and so pushing away. Push and pull. Of merging and rejecting. Of loving and hating and fearing. A person with borderline personality disorder is not born, but made (Robinson, 2003), through the social interactions with those around them and life events they have experienced in combination with certain innate propensities such as personality traits and abilities to manage stress. Working with endings is a central part of the therapy, especially when this plays out as abandonment. My patients often witnessed events in which they felt helplessness and hopelessness as children and young adults, and now manage their lives as best as they have learned how. Regardless of the label of borderline personality disorder, my patients made and make the best of their lives, they survived the chaos of their youth and acted in the most authentic way they could in the 'here and now'. For that, my patients will always have my most profound respect.

Diagnosis only makes sense in a relationship, in the minutiae of a relationship between two people. Otherwise, the jargon of a diagnosis is simply empty words which are themselves abandoning of a person. Receiving a diagnosis from upon high, from behind a desk, from a chair opposite, from behind a clipboard, from behind a computer screen, can be as isolating as it could be liberating. Abandonment can be experienced when no context is given. A diagnosis needs a relationship to make it three dimensional. I work with diagnosis; it can be a signpost I choose to consider with the patient. Abandonment and an inner sense of emptiness are particularly pertinent to the diagnosis of borderline personality disorder, and play out in the ending of therapy.

In this chapter endings have been considered in relation to breaks and gifts and the profound meanings evident in them. It is these meanings that remind us that diagnosis is a list of the dysfunctional defensive outcomes and not the true core wounds of the patient. So when working with patients who may have such a diagnosis, remember that feared rejection and abandonment is about self and other love. I would suggest you risk letting your patients love you and hate you and explore and prepare the end with them. What you make of the ending can be shared with patients when it feels right. Ends are a marker in the relationship and the marker needs to be acknowledged.

References

American Psychiatric Association (1994). *Diagnostic and Statistical Manual of Mental Disorders* (4th ed). Washington, DC: American Psychiatric Association.

Astley, N (2002). *Staying Alive: Real poems for unreal times.* Northumberland: Bloodaxe.

Auerbach, JS & Blatt, SJ (1996). Self-representation in severe psychopathology: The role of reflexive self-awareness. *Psychoanalytic Psychology, 13,* 297–341.

Becker, D & Lamb, S (1994). Sex bias in the diagnosis of borderline personality disorder and posttraumatic stress disorder. *Professional Psychology: Research and Practice, 25,* 55–61.

Casement, P (1985). *On Learning from the Patient*. Hove: Routledge.

Coid, J, Yang, M, Tyrer, P, Roberts, A & Ullrich, S (2006). Prevalence and correlates of personality disorder in Great Britain. *British Journal of Psychiatry, 188,* 423–31.

Dazzi, S (1998). Some thoughts concerning borderline pathology and fear of aloneness. *Journal of the American Academy of Psychoanalysis, 26,* 69–84.

De Moor, MHM, Distel, MA, Trull, TJ & Boomsma, DI (2009). Assessment of borderline personality features in population samples: Is the Personality Assessment Inventory-Borderline Features scale measurement invariant across sex and age? *Psychological Assessment, 21,* 125–30.

Fleming, J (1975). Some observations on object constancy in the psychoanalysis of adults. *Journal of the American Psychoanalytic Association, 23,* 743–59.

Fonagy, P (1989). On tolerating mental states: Theory of mind in borderline personality. *Bulletin of the Anna Freud Centre, 12,* 91–115.

Fonagy, P (1993). Psychoanalytic and empirical approaches to developmental psychopathology: An object-relations perspective. *Research in Psychoanalysis: Process, development & outcome, 41,* 245–60.

Fonagy, P (2000). Attachment and borderline personality disorder. *Journal of the American Psychoanalytic Association, 48,* 1129–46.

Fonagy, P, Gergely, G, Jurist, EL & Target, M (2007). *Affect Regulation, Mentalisation and the Development of the Self.* London: Karnac.

Ford, MR & Widiger, TA (1989). Sex bias in the diagnosis of histrionic and antisocial personality disorders. *Journal of Consulting and Clinical Psychology, 57,* 301–5.

Foucault, M (1980). *Power/Knowledge: Selected interviews and other writings 1972–1997.* Brighton: Harvester Press.

Hartung, CM & Widiger, TA (1998). Gender differences in the diagnosis of mental disorders: Conclusions and controversies of the *DSM-IV. Psychological Bulletin, 123,* 260–78.

Hoagland, T (2003). *What Narcissism Means to Me.* Minneapolis, MN: Graywolf Press.

Garb, HN (1995). Sex bias and the diagnosis of borderline personality disorder. *Professional Psychology: Research and Practice, 27,* 272–7.

Garb, HN (1997). Race bias, social class bias, and gender bias in clinical judgement. *Clinical Psychology: Science and Practice, 4,* 99–120.

Gottlieb, MC, Younggren, JN & Murch, KB (2009). Boundary management for cognitive behavioral therapies. *Cognitive and Behavioral Practice, 16,* 164–71.

Johnson, DM, Shea, MT, Yen, S, Battle, CL, Zlotnick, C, Sanislow, CA, et al. (2003). Gender differences in borderline personality disorder: Findings from the collaborative longitudinal personality disorders study. *Comprehensive Psychiatry, 44,* 284–92.

Lenzenweger, MF, Lane, MC, Loranger, AW & Kessler, RC (2007). *DSM-IV* personality disorders in the National Comorbidity Survey Replication. *Biological Psychiatry, 62,* 187–96.

Leo, RJ & Cartagena, MT (1999). Gender bias in psychiatric texts. *Academic Psychiatry, 23,* 71–6.

Linehan, MM (1993). *Cognitive-Behavioural Treatment of Borderline Personality Disorder*. New York: Guilford Press.

Lowe, R (1999). Between the 'no longer' and the 'not yet': Postmodernism as a context for critical therapeutic work. In I Parker (Ed) *Deconstructing Psychotherapy*. London: Sage.

Maier, W, Lichtermann, D, Klingler, T, Heun, R & Hallmayer, J (1992). Prevalences of personality disorders (*DSM-III-R*) in the community. *Journal of Personality Disorders, 6,* 187–96.

Maitland, K (2008). *Company of Liars*. London: Penguin Books.

Morey, LC & Ochoa, ES (1989). An investigation of adherence to diagnostic criteria: Clinical diagnosis of the *DSM-III* personality disorders. *Journal of Personality Disorders, 3,* 180–92.

Proctor, G (2003). CBT: Collaboration or compliance? *Clinical Psychology, 25*, 14–16.

Richman, NE & Sokolove, RL (1992). The experience of aloneness, object representation, and evocative memory in borderline and neurotic patients. *Psychoanalytic Psychology, 9,* 77–91.

Robinson, DJ (2003). *The Personality Disorders Explained* (2nd ed). Port Huron, MI: Rapid Psychler Press.

Spinelli, E (2006). *Demystifying Therapy* (reprinted ed). Ross-on-Wye: PCCS Books.

Torgersen, S, Kringlen, E, & Cramer, V (2001). The prevalence of personality disorders in a community sample. *Archives of General Psychiatry, 58*, 590–6.

Wallston, BS & Grady, KE (1985). Integrating the feminist critique and the crisis in social psychology: Another look at research methods. In VE O'Leary, RK Unger & BS Wallston (Eds) *Women, Gender and Social Psychology*. Hillside, NJ: Erlbaum.

Weinberg, E (2006). Mentalization, affect regulation and development of the self. *Journal of the American Psychoanalytic Association, 54,* 251–70.

Widiger, TA & Trull, TJ (1993). Borderline and narcissistic personality disorders. In P Sutker & H Adams (Eds) *Comprehensive Textbook of Psychopathology* (2nd ed). New York: Plenum Press.

Winnicott, DW (1959). The fate of the transitional object. In C Winnicott, R Shepherd & M Davis (Eds) *Psychoanalytic Explorations: D. W. Winnicott* (2nd ed). Harvard, MA: Harvard University Press.

Winnicott, DW (1991). *The Child, the Family and the Outside World* (3rd ed). London: Penguin Books.

Winnicott, DW (2005). *Playing and Reality* (9th ed). London: Routledge.

Winnicott, DW (2007). *Through Paediatrics to Psychoanalysis* (9th ed). London: Karnac.

Woodward, HE, Taft, CT, Gordon, RA & Meis, LA (2009). Clinician bias in the diagnosis of posttraumatic stress disorder and borderline personality disorder. *Psychological Trauma: Theory, Research, Practice and Policy, 1,* 282–90.

Author's note

Tim Knowlson would like to thank and acknowledge the following authors, poets and representatives of publishing houses for permission to include quotations in his chapter:

Karen Maitland and Rachel Atkinson at Penguin Books Ltd for permission to publish the excerpt from *Company of Liars* (page 487).

R.S. Thomas and Dr Suzanne Fairless-Aitken at Bloodaxe Books Ltd for permission to publish the excerpt from *The Cry*.

Tony Hoagland and Frederick T. Courtright at Graywolf Ltd for permission to publish the excerpt from *What Narcissism Means to Me*.

8

Embodiment and Somatoform Distress: From symptoms to domains

Ben Rumble

Welcome!
(Lessons from Levinas, 1999 and Derrida, 2000)

Come! You are welcome. Come as you are, as other. I'm at your disposal. All I know, my relative expertise, is available for you. Here's my formulation – take it please! I'll give you something of what I know, but what I cannot presume to know is you. It's true, I'm continually curious and bothered by you, but I can do no more than welcome and allow you to arrive. Hopefully there is warmth, trust and intimacy to our relationship. But also divergence, separation. The point isn't simply to get on. Our relationship is never straightforward. We zig and we zag. At times you are familiar, close by, and we'll tarry along together; at times you're distant and unfamiliar, far away. Always synchrony tempered by diachrony. This is how we spend our time together. Both are welcome. Let's keep to this separation so that we might be surprised. Sharing surprise is the best way to meet. Perhaps all I can do is welcome surprise. Strange reversal. I take you on and wait to be overtaken. Surprised, I might make links and perhaps share them with you. Take them and I'll try to expect nothing in return. Let's keep to this relationship, this unpredictable rhythm of surprise and intimacy; this might be the best outcome we can hope for.

In welcoming I'm taken hostage by you. I'm overtaken. For the next 50 minutes you have my attention, quite literally. You have it. I have little or no choice in the matter. Everything which comes to mind is in relation to you and your company. I try to notice my being taken hostage, notice what is occurring, mediate a little but not too much. If I begin to leave, drift off, notice this. If I can't leave and I'm transfixed, notice this too. Everything which comes to mind is in relation and everything I might do is in relation – the smallest gesture, shift in posture, stomach growl, impulse to sneeze. Nothing is involuntary. Everything gathers significance in your company. Yet the way I'm taken hostage is more than simply a matter of attention and behaviour. The scene for this hostage taking is one of incarnation. You have me in my skin. An odd phrase I know. But your proximity is not just a matter of feet and inches, nor am I simply under your gaze. It's so much more than this. When you are nearby I'm overtaken *in* my body. I'm constricted in my skin. I'm hemmed in, caught, incarnated *into* this relationship. I'm not sure of a better way to say this. In welcoming you, I give up something of *my* body, the freedom to move of my own accord, so that I might be moved in your company. Something is spirited away, dispossessed, temporarily replaced. Soft coup – benign takeover. Perhaps I should put a sign on the door: 'Departure and arrival. Waiting room this way, departures and arrivals over here.'

So in welcoming you, I try to follow this body which takes place, go with it, arrive with it. This body, this dispossession, belongs to us. It's ours but not to keep. It comes and goes. I try to be in two places at once. Try to notice things arrive and depart, appear and disappear – quickly, slowly, gently or forcefully. Try to mediate and steer a little, but not too much. Notice 'my' body being nudged to one side, constricted, moved by your company. This takes practice. Waiting for you to arrive I might sit quietly and see what's around. Thoughts and associations approach but also sensations. An outline or image assembles, my body felt from within, composed, coherent, familiar, safe. I tuck myself into this emerging sense of body, locate myself there; settle into the composure and stillness on offer. This is often how I sit with you: back straight, head slightly down and to the left, eyes slightly towards you, hand on hand, folded, receptive. I don't so much sit down as arrive into the archipelago of a therapist's body. Yet even on the inside you're already there, in the neighbourhood. The assembled composure simply gives the lie to my already having been disturbed. You got here before me, but at least now I'm *ready* to be disturbed. Here I am, now I can leave; welcome, I'm ready to be overtaken (see Cooper, 2009; Derrida, 2000; Levinas, 1999).

Therapeutic setting and diagnostic milieu

The welcome I seek to offer the client must take place somewhere. And the name for this place is the therapeutic setting, wherever that might be (Spurling, 2004). As with any form of hospitality, the setting comes with house rules which carefully limit and specify the kind of welcome on offer (Derrida, 2000; Spurling, 2004). The setting's boundary effectively establishes a dwelling place from which to offer therapy. It is by keeping to the boundary of place, time and contract that the client is able to become and remain a client and cross the threshold of therapy, whilst I can become and remain the therapist and welcome the client across the threshold. The containing power of this boundary is often commented on (Spurling, 2004). But the boundary also increases the force and affirmation of the welcome on offer – Come! For the next 50 minutes you have my undivided attention. You have me in my skin. The boundedness of therapy increases the sense of takeover, of willingly being held hostage by the other.

Understanding the relationship between therapy and place is important because applied psychology is often nomadic, moving between GP surgeries, or finding a place for therapy in a busy psychiatric hospital, for example. As I arrange the chairs for a session or tack the sign 'please do not disturb' to the door, I'm aware of 'setting up shop', of marking out the parameters of a particular kind of interaction, a specific kind of welcome which can be called therapy. I'm also aware that even as I set a place for therapy, I am myself a guest within what could be described as a diagnostic milieu (see Hinshelwood, 2001) – an institution, such as a GP surgery or hospital, which is founded on the classification and treatment of disease. Now the tension between diagnosis and psychotherapy is well known and, arguably, hinges on the value which psychotherapy places on relationship (Harvey et al., 2004; Strawbridge & Woolfe, 2003). Whilst diagnosis understands human distress in terms of symptoms, disease categories and treatable objective disorders, the process of psychotherapy is an 'implicit relational knowing' which is often unspoken and mediated moment by moment (Beebe & Lachmann, 2002; Boston Change Process Group, 1998; Harvey et al., 2004).

Where diagnosis seeks separation, light and decision, relational knowing accepts messiness, glimmerings and uncertainty. Yet to focus on diagnosis solely as a way of knowing at odds with relationship is to forget that diagnosis is also a place (Foucault, 1973). Diagnosis is where I work. Applying psychology in a psychiatric hospital or GP surgery, I'm in the midst of diagnosis, within and surrounded by diagnosis. As I walk along hospital corridors, passing different departments, oncology, phlebotomy, maternity, I'm aware that the architecture itself is a form of classification which separates, sifts and excludes (Foucault, 1973.). I work amongst stethoscopes, scanners, blood pressure kits, equipment to detect symptoms and objectify distress. I work alongside nurses, psychiatrists, occupational therapists, GPs – colleagues who might firmly believe in the existence of distinct treatable disorders and consider diagnosis as an appropriate way of understanding distress. I welcome 'clients' whose arrival into the hospital or GP waiting room presupposes a diagnostic threshold which establishes them as 'patients'. To set a place for therapy within a diagnostic milieu therefore requires careful negotiation, a politics of diagnosis even. To leave diagnosis at the door of therapy is to forget where I work and whom I work with, a politically irresponsible act. It follows that welcoming diagnosis to therapy should be tempered by an ethical commitment to go beyond diagnosis to the client; to welcome trust, respect, warmth, alterity, mutuality, unknowing, surprise; all the values, then, which dwell within therapy and motivate working in relationship (Woolfe, Dryden & Strawbridge, 2003).

Between hostage and statue

For the remainder of this chapter I'd like to trace a route around diagnosis which pays particular attention to the body. The background to this venture is the Levinasian (1999) idea that in welcoming the client I'm taken hostage in my body. Welcoming is incarnation. You have me in my skin. I'm hemmed in, incarnated into *this* relationship. This sense of proximity in which the other is not so much over there as right on the body – right on the boundary between self and other, confusing, bothering, constricting – might be described as the extreme point of relationship. The point at which there is nothing to do, think or say except affirm the therapeutic encounter. Welcome! We can imagine this extreme point as the beginning of a continuum, the other end of which might be the separation, light and knowing of diagnosis.

When the other has me in my skin, the body is all constriction and confusion, a restlessness which can only be affirmed. Diagnosis reverses this perspective and places the other at an observable distance. Diagnosis sends the other away. No longer in my skin, the other is over there, visible, immobilised, isolated, the relationship between our bodies severed. Medically speaking, the purpose of this way of seeing is to separate and objectify the body as a possible site of disease (Foucault, 1973). Within psychiatric nosology, however, the objectified body becomes a demarcation point from which to gauge psychopathology (Aho & Aho, 2008; Foucault, 1973; Rumble, 2009). For example, the person who repeatedly states 'I have cancer' may be diagnosed with health anxiety if the statement refers to a body which, medically speaking is in good heath. The person who repeatedly states 'I am overweight' may have anorexia if the statement refers to a body which, objectively speaking, is underweight. The objective body highlights a possible psychological problem and in doing so implicitly devalues or at least disconfirms the client's experience of the body which they feel themselves to be. The price of diagnosis, then, is the 'lived body' (see Aho & Aho, 2008; Merleau-Ponty, 1962). Small wonder the client complains of theft and replies 'you've stolen my body' (see Artaud, 1992). And this is no Cartesian quibble. The line between objective body and disordered mind is powerfully drawn and includes the potential to be literally sent away, separated, sectioned (Foucault, 1989; Milner & Rose, 1986).

The psychologist's reticence with respect to diagnosis lies with the more tentative goals of formulation and explanation (Grant et al., 2008). The difficulty here is that while psychological science has developed in a direction which increasingly brings body and mind together (Damasio, 2006; Gallagher, 2005; Lakoff & Johnson, 1999; Varela et al., 1993), all too often applied psychological therapy casts light on the client's mind at the expense of their body. While in the lab psyche and soma are becoming synonymous, in the clinic the body can get left out, treated as an object devoid of subjectivity. For example, if we consider the origins of psychotherapy, the role of the body in conversion disorder is conceived as a container for the unwanted contents of the mind (Freud & Breuer, 2004). More recently, body dysmorphic disorder is explained as an attentional bias which distorts the client's experience of what, objectively speaking, is an unblemished body (Cash, 2002). The difference between psychodynamic and cognitive therapy in this context is only one of degree with both modalities, at least in their traditional forms, serving to divide the client into an active constituting mind and a more passive constituted body.

The hypothesis I shall now explore is as follows: 'what if the body possessed a life and a mind of its own?' More specifically, what if body movement was not simply a physiological process but a living intention which meant something? Movements could be conceived as relationships which connect things up, like so many bridges, creating mini-neighbourhoods, dwellings, milieux. No longer a passive object, the body could be conceived as an agent of some sort, an intensive event which sweeps through a particular place in a particular way at a particular time. And if this were the case then psychological formulation would have to include the body and provide a map of the various relationships which characterise a milieu. The bones of this hypothesis are scattered throughout the work of Merleau-Ponty (1962), Deleuze and Guattari (1994) and enactive cognitive science (Thompson, 2007), and are beginning to influence how psychological therapy approaches distress (Diamond, 2001; Fuchs et al., 2010; Molbak, 2007; Rumble, 2010). What unites these distinct approaches is the idea that the body is not only an object but a particular kind of subjectivity, broadly termed embodiment. In drawing on these approaches, I shall characterise embodiment as consisting of three key elements: movement, affect and domains. Embodiment occupies a middle ground between the body as hostage to the therapeutic encounter and the more distant, frozen object of diagnosis. If we can get the embodiment hypothesis to stand up and walk, the challenge is then to provide formulation which includes the body and so is wholly on the side of the client.

Useful example

Let's start with a simple example which draws on the phenomenological observations of Merleau-Ponty (1962) and mindful awareness (Segal et al., 2002). Stand still with your hands by your sides in front of the object or objects which compose a familiar action; this could be a door, a chair, a kettle, pen and paper, anything you like. Now, whilst standing still, close your eyes and begin to scan your body from head to toe: sense your current position, your posture; sense the weight and volume of your frame, the space your body takes up; make room for your body and allow an image of your body to arrive. Inhabit this image, settle in, sense it. Now open your eyes and focus on the object, the door, pen or kettle, whilst also paying attention to your motionless body. Consider the relationship between your body and the object, the potential action which might emerge. Notice how the object seems to call on your body; the way a vector or line of force runs between your body and the object, marking out the potential route you might take. Correspondingly, your motionless body seems to respond to the object's call as a kind of simmering on the spot. Your body is ready for the door, the pen, the kettle. You might even sense the beginnings of a movement, a phantom arm reaching out for the object. Now reach out for the object. Lean into and allow the movement to happen. Open the door, pick up the pen. Notice how the action unfolds in a single movement which spans your whole body, from the tip of your fingers to the soles of your feet. Each shift in posture is felt throughout the body as a whole. And notice that as you lean into the movement your body corresponds with the object. Even as you reach for the door handle, the pen, the kettle, your body anticipates and adjusts to the object's shape and potential weight. Too fast, too slow, too much, too little and you and the object will fall out. Always adjustment, dialogue, flow. This is how we move.

Couples, spirals, domains

If we now flesh out this brief interaction with a vocabulary drawn from enactive cognitive science (Thompson, 2007) we can say the following. In calling up a movement, the object possesses a meaning which appeals directly to the body. More specifically, the door handle is a 'salient' feature which immediately stands out to the hand. In responding to this appeal, through reaching and opening, the meaning is 'enacted' (ibid.). Meaning in this context is not an abstract cognition but an action in which handle and hand form a meaningful unit or 'couple'. Coupling doesn't simply happen out of the blue but emerges as an ongoing 'sense-making dialogue' between the body and its surroundings (ibid.). For example, the hand doesn't mechanically grab but anticipates and adjusts to the handle to create the movement which is just right for this particular object. Similarly, when viewing a picture for the first time we don't see the image in one go but move back and forth until the viewpoint emerges which makes sense, the view which feels right for this particular picture (Merleau-Ponty, 1962). The sense-making dialogue is a circular interaction of adjustment and co-ordination, tension and resolution. Things are effectively questions to which the body replies 'like this?', 'is this the body you mean?' Actions are intentions, expectations, which respond to salient features and seek an optimum grip on a given situation (Merleau-Ponty, 1962; Thompson, 2007).

Sense making creates 'domains' (Thompson, 2007). A domain is what happens in the vicinity of a body, the shadow which movement casts on our surroundings. A domain is not so much a defined place as a kind of overlap or neighbourhood; a region of significance which we inhabit with a specific orientation or expectation (Deleuze, 1970; Thompson, 2007). Of course the preceding example was an artificial one. No one just opens a door. The door leads somewhere, somebody walks in. So imagine the door leads to a betting shop. A gambler enters followed by a non-gambler. One shop, two domains. The non-gambler leaves, indifferent. The gambler remains, alert, responsive, coupled to the TV, the betting slip, the pencil, the cashier. Domains consist of 'salient' and 'valent' features which stand out to and galvanise the body (see Lewin, 1936; Thompson, 2007). These features are like so many dots which the body encircles and joins together. The body is a little like a stylus which spirals back and forth, this way and that, from feature to feature to feature, sketching out the routes and couplings that go to fill a particular domain (see Deleuze, 1968; Thompson, 2007).

Domains are meeting points, overlaps, haunts; vicinities comprised of couplings, selections and orientations; the vectors followed and routes taken towards, away, around and through things (Deleuze, 1970; Thompson, 2007). The kind of domain which emerges depends entirely on *how* the coupling takes place (Thompson, 2007). A specific kind of body sketches a specific kind of domain. A tense, angry body composed of forceful, stubborn movement generates a world of slamming doors, splintered objects, blown fuses. Body and surroundings mutually specify each other so that an angry body generates and inhabits an angry world, an anxious body, an anxious world, a threatened body, a threatening world. The relationship between body and surroundings is therefore never neutral. At any given time we are enveloped by various levels or degrees of salience or relevance and various levels or degrees of valence or attraction (Deleuze, 1968; Thompson, 2007). Orientation and arousal are therefore central to how our surroundings gel together and make sense. It follows that although domains are *where* we tend to end up, strictly speaking a domain is an event. A domain is a selection, an affective threshold, something which becomes relevant at a certain point (Deleuze, 1970). And as such domains can come and go – seemingly pressing, intrusive or suddenly irrelevant, distant, far away.

Dynamic movement

The immediate coupling of handle and hand illustrates the dynamic role movement plays in generating domains. The body's dynamism arises from the multiple *potential* connections which can arise between 'distinctive points' (Deleuze, 1968), such as arms, hands, legs and feet, and environmental features. Combining points and features then gathers the potential connections into coherent domain-specific movements (see Deleuze, 1968; Merleau-Ponty, 1962; Thelen & Smith, 1996). For example, I don't simply see the approaching ball so much as I sense the approach through my body's preparation for the catch. The high jumper's steady focus on the bar assembles the body about to jump into the movement which will carry her over. Our potential for movement is a potential to connect points and features. Coupling then translates this potential into domain-specific abilities, such as jumping or catching.

Whether jumping, catching, approaching or withdrawing, movements are never pieced together move by move, but gather and unfold in one go, galvanised by this or that (Merleau-Ponty, 1962). Movements happen in sections which abut and build on each other as the body progressively couples with domain-specific features. We can now add a useful Deleuzian idea (1970). These sections then intersect to create an overall 'plane' which is *moved through* when inhabiting a domain (ibid.). Domains sit on planes. For example, teapot, cup and spoon couple with pouring and stirring to make tea. Movement isn't so much something we do as something we *go through* to do what we do. From teapot to cup, through pouring and stirring, to do anything we need to get going, get onto a movement plane consisting of coupled points and features. It is this overall plane which the high jumper seems to catch hold of at the start of the jump. The jumper initially sways, seemingly in mid-movement, as her body assembles and catches hold of the route she steps straight onto.

A power of inhabitation

What is it like to inhabit a domain? The in-one-go-ness of movement is such that each shift in the body interconnects with its neighbour, forming melodic lines which move throughout the body (Merleau-Ponty, 1962). Whether catching, jumping or making tea, movement forms the basis for a kinaesthetic sense of self which is potentially fluid, bounded and coherent (Krueger, 1989; Merleau-Ponty, 1962; Sheets-Johnstone, 1999) – such is the comfort of habit. However, because the body's potential is ultimately a potential to connect, new movements can always emerge, new combinations, new domains, new ways of being. We can see this in sport with the transition from scissor jump to Fosbury flop, from breast stroke to crawl, long jump to triple jump (Deleuze, 1997). And in daily life, learning a new skill can reassemble and set the body on a new trajectory, a new way of meeting the world.

Deleuze's (1970) distinction between domain and plane is helpful in explaining how change can happen. Domains are concentrated couplings which sit on a movement plane. Because the plane is constructed section by section, coupled feature by coupled feature, the plane is never completely closed, but can always branch off (ibid.). So while domains are fairly fixed tendencies, the plane is essentially plastic, open to new combinations. Domains are connections but the plane is the capacity to connect. To learn something new is to shed or transform a domain and so move along the plane towards something else. If we remember that movement isn't something we do so much as something we *go through* to do what we do, then we can think of the body as adrift on a movement plane. Domains are like so many eddies or mini whirlpools which we can pass through or get caught up in (see Varela et al., 1993).

These aspects of bodily dynamism – coherence and potential – can be combined if we consider the body as a *felt power* of inhabitation; that sense of yourself as able to occupy and move between domains (Merleau-Ponty, 1962; Rumble, 2009). This feeling of power concerns both bodily know-how and, importantly, intensive variations in arousal and valence (Deleuze, 1970; Thompson, 2007). Stepping into my car, the instrument panel immediately appeals to a series of free flowing movements relating to my ability to drive. 'Mirror, signal, manoeuvre' is not a meaningless repetition of a habit learnt whilst still a teenager, but my body's continuing to couple with the car's salient features. I move through the milieu simply because *I can*, because the car has immediate sense and value which galvanises my body into action. However, following a road traffic accident this felt power might atrophy. Although I still know how to drive, the car becomes a threat which is reflected in my bodily being. I can still sense the direction of the car's salient features, but my ability to get going stultifies as my body oscillates between anxious rigidity and dishevelled incoherence. In a way the trauma leaves me stuck to the threshold of a domain. My sense of direction is intact but I can't connect. I'm missing the plane, the point by point which can carry me through (see Ogden, Minton & Pain, 2006).

Our power of inhabitation is something which can expand and contract and can correspond to increasingly limited or disorganised domains. How then to provide a coherent yet parsimonious analysis of this power? Deleuze (1970) suggests we analyse the body along two axes, one spatial and one intensive. The co-ordinates of the spatial axis are the neighbouring points and features which might characterise a domain. The intensive axis concerns the variations in arousal which characterise precisely *how* someone inhabits and moves through a domain (Deleuze, 1970; Deleuze & Guattari, 1994). The spatial axis sets the *potential* scene for a domain. The intensity axis sets the domain threshold, the level of arousal at which a domain happens. Once a threshold is reached the intensity axis then crosses the spatial axis like a wave, connecting points and features, condensing them into the intensive ordinates which characterise a singular way of being (Deleuze & Guattari, 1994). The two axes provide something to grab hold of when analysing a domain and remind us that going through a domain is always also a passage through the ups and downs of a feeling.

Intersubjectivity

Stick out your tongue at a newborn infant and the baby may well mirror the gesture and you'll want to mirror it straight back (Trevarthen & Aitkin, 2001). From birth our bodies tend to co-ordinate and move together, creating couples and social groups (Gallagher, 2005). The salient and valent features which pave the way for this co-ordination are many and can focus on face, eyes, limbs, smiles, head turns, leans, eyebrows, gestures and voice tone (Beebe & Lachmann, 2002; Stern, 1985; Trevarthen & Aitkin, 2001). Smiles initiate smiles, gestures interlink, couples form. Social features reciprocally determine each other, creating an interactive plane, no matter how brief. Couples then move along the plane in varying states of mutuality and synchrony (De Jaegher & Di Paulo, 2007; Fuchs & De Jaegher, 2010). The interaction's intensive ordinates concern affects and their attunement (Stern, 1985, 2010). A child quickly, angrily, throws down a toy. The carer matches the movement's force, but then slows and gently returns the toy. The child giggles. Deceleration, soft landing. Quickness meets quickness and then slows; harshness meets harshness and softens. Loudness meets loudness and quietens. Tension rises and melts away. The rhythmic interaction is a game of matching and modulating affects; of meeting and moving along intensive gradients, through thresholds and across levels (Deleuze, 1968; Stern, 1985, 2010). What is an affect if not something to ascend or descend through? Affects have as much depth and topography as a landscape. So when the carer responds it is as if one body says to another: 'I can see you're getting stuck, stuck in a feeling, but look this is how we move, follow me; I'll meet your fierceness but here's how to quieten, to soften and soothe. Here's how to move up or down, here's how to leave.' Bodies call on each other, seeking and expecting a rhythmic complement or counterpoint; a threshold or route through, a way out. 'Help, I'm getting stuck.' 'This way, follow me.' One body in the vicinity of another. Roles and responses are evoked (Ryle & Kerr, 2002; Sandler, 1976). Expectations crowd in. Scary and scared bodies, caring and cared-for bodies, tensing and tensed bodies. We meet at a bottleneck of bodies.

A typology and topology of embodied distress

Let's try and draw this analysis towards a couple of clinically salient points. Rather than focus on symptoms and discrete diagnostic categories, an embodied approach might conceptualise distress as a particular way of generating and inhabiting domains (Fuchs, 2010; Rumble, 2010). The body is not an isolated object but a power of inhabitation. This capacity can range from a concentrated set of bodily habits corresponding to a limited milieu, through to a more diffuse or incoherent sense of body, which corresponds to a distant or perhaps intrusive milieu (Fuchs 2005; Rumble, 2010; Weiss, 1999). We all pass along this spectrum every day. Consider the difference between the concentrated habits of early morning – cleaning teeth, making tea – which carry you quickly from milieu to milieu, from bathroom, to breakfast, to car. And compare these to the more drowsy diffusion of late evening when objects lose their appeal and slip away, or suddenly intrude and persist. The car horn at midday was a distraction, last thing at night it makes you jump.

Distress happens when our capacity to generate, inhabit and move between domains becomes progressively concentrated or diffused (Fuchs, 2010; Merleau-Ponty, 1962; Rumble, 2010; Weiss, 1999). The circular relationship between body and milieu is such that we can then get stuck into increasingly limited or disorganised domains. This progressive immersion is then accompanied by a kind of domain drift (see Varela et al., 1993) as the individual moves away from shared, intersubjective domains and into a distress-based milieu (Fuchs, 2010; Rumble, 2010). Distress is a crossing of some sort. An intensive threshold is reached and suddenly we are in the vicinity of something: food, a skin blemish, a voice, some germs. This movement suggests that distress crosses a 'transdiagnostic' continuum (Harvey et al., 2004) ranging from a concentrated to a diffused power of inhabitation. For example, the focused mileux of obsessive-compulsive disorder (OCD), anorexia and body dysmorphic disorder (BDD) might gather at the more concentrated end of the spectrum (Rumble, 2010; Weiss, 1999). The distant or intrusive milieux of depression and schizophrenia might gather at the more diffused end of the spectrum (Fuchs, 2005, 2010;

Rumble, 2010). Perhaps certain presentations (panic, social anxiety, post-traumatic stress disorder (PTSD), bi-polar disorder) traverse both ends as concentration switches to diffusion and back.

Bodies sketch and inhabit domains. Distressed bodies sketch distressing domains. The point, then, is not to simply fit existing diagnostic categories to a continuum, but to approach distress on a case-by-case basis beginning with the question, 'what kind of domain is happening here?' For example, PTSD might generate a world of sudden jolts and aggressive intrusions, which correspond to a frozen, fearful body (Ogden et al., 2006). Depression creates a world of distant objects and blunted valance, which correspond to a diffuse and heavy body (Fuchs, 2005). It follows that distress is not a property of anything, be it the individual, the environment, cognition, behaviour etc. Distress is no more than a relationship. A potential orientation on a plane composed of points and features (see Deleuze, 2006). The genesis of distress lies in the intensive coupling of these points and features to create domains. Inhabiting and repeatedly going through a domain maintains the distress and progressively separates the individual from shared domains. We get caught in domains at the expense of the plastic open plane. This isn't to say that domain drift is necessarily antisocial in nature. Because domains are not defined places but overlaps or vicinities, a domain can always get lodged in or next to some other domain. Consequently, borderline personality disorder (BPD) might be understood as the drift into concentrated, idiosyncratic ways of relating which are lodged within social domains.

A distress spectrum, ranging from a concentrated to a diffused power of inhabitation, is the broadest stroke, a simple typology which might provide the clinician with an initial perspective on a presentation. Formulation, however, means returning to the events. What might be described as a topological formulation (see Lewin, 1936) could be created by following Deleuze's (1970) suggestion and plotting the spatial co-ordinates and intensive ordinates of a distressing event. Spatial co-ordinates concern the overlapping points and features which set out the topology of a potential domain. Intensive ordinates mark the threshold at which a domain happens and the affective phases which characterise how the individual goes through a domain. For example, working with self-harm might be guided by the idea that self-harm behaviour is animated by the immediate co-ordination of hand to salient implement. This coupling is accompanied by distinct intensive phases: rising agitation ☐ coupling of point and feature ☐ cutting sensation ☐ calm. Whilst the function of self-harm might well be to regulate arousal (Walsh, 2005), a domain-based approach emphasises that arousal is always selection and orientation. In other words, feelings *take place*. The genesis of self-harm might therefore lie with the progressive coupling of points and features to create a self-harming milieu – a space in which it becomes possible to literally go through a feeling. The maintenance of self-harm then lies with the immediate co-ordination with and movement through a milieu whenever certain intensive thresholds are reached.

A topological formulation might attempt to capture this movement to provide a sense of something you go through – an event which happens quick as a flash: the high jumper's leap, mirror–signal–manoeuvre, the hand that cuts, a washing ritual. Whilst the importance of domains is already implicit in CBT's emphasis on safety behaviour, for example, attending to the intensity of a domain means introducing a vocabulary which is largely absent from traditional psychotherapy. Words like shrinking/growing, quickening/slowing, freezing/melting, hardening/softening, rising/falling become important – words which can sensitise and empower the client to notice the affective gradients and thresholds which characterise their distress (Stern, 2010). Spatial co-ordinates and intensive ordinates can then plot a real-time diagram of the distress event. For example, habitual self-harm might consist of a single point–feature orientation with two intensive ordinates (Figure 1).

Figure 1: A self-harm domain

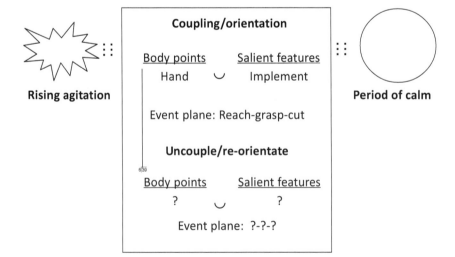

The idea is not to create an exhaustive cross section, but simply a sketch, a few key components which might provide a sense of how distress gathers and unfolds; a sense of 'as-if-ness' or 'about-to-ness' which might dramatise an event. As with any dramatised event, going through the diagram can then assist the client to develop a sense of direction and perhaps anticipate rather than simply go through an action. The diagram can then be used to consider possible exit points. Figure 1 offers two exit points: the first involves shifting the domain's intensive threshold by modulating arousal, through mindful breathing (Segal et al., 2002; McKay et al., 2007), for example. The second might involve setting out a new milieu composed of different salient/valent features.

A domain-based approach would highlight that mindful affect regulation alone is insufficient as the client would still be left in the vicinity of a self-harm domain. The key, therefore, is to construct a new coupling able to facilitate the transition from agitation to calm. This doesn't simply mean substituting an alternative behaviour which is less harmful. The point is to carefully consider and mindfully follow the appeal of new salient/valent features to allow a divergent duration and movement to emerge. The intervention is not so much a substitution as a kind of shading or overlapping of the current distress milieu. For example, the client who habitually self-harms might have the co-ordinates of an alternative domain set up and waiting. A domain-based approach might therefore lie in carefully uncoupling the concentrated habits of OCD, anorexia or self-harm, for example, creating exit points and offshoots to other potential milieus (see Deusund & Skarderud, 2003). Similarly the diffusion of depression or schizophrenia might be reduced by facilitating new habits which effectively re-embody the client, facilitating increased co-ordination and engagement (see De Haan & Fuchs, 2010). The rationale at both ends of the spectrum is to initiate drift, to extend the event plane away from concentrated or diffused couplings towards other potential interactions.

Summary and conclusion

This chapter began with a single word, welcome. Welcoming is incarnation. To welcome the client is to be willingly held hostage in your own skin. This Levinasian (1999) idea can be regarded as the extreme point of relationship, nothing other than relationship. No words, no thoughts, only an affirmative '… yes to the other' (Derrida, 2007). Diagnosis sends the other away.

Diagnosis is dis-incarnation. The other is known, held at a distance, encased in symptoms and categories. This knowing is sometimes necessary, politically unavoidable, often of assistance to the client, but should be tempered by a yes to the other as other; yes to the confusion, constriction and bothersomeness of the therapeutic encounter. In between skin and diagnosis lies embodiment. A model of embodiment is then provided which draws on Merleau-Ponty (1962), enactive cognitive science (Thompson, 2007) and Deleuze and Guattari (1994).

Merleau-Ponty and enactive cognitive science contributed the idea that the body is not simply an object but a lived capacity to generate and inhabit meaningful domains. Domains consist of salient and valent features which we approach with a particular orientation and expectation. Deleuze and Guattari contributed a second affective dimension, the intensive thresholds and phases which characterise precisely how we combine with and pass through a domain. A domain is not so much a place as an overlap, a vicinity, a particular affect at a particular time, which can come and go. Following Deleuze's (1970) suggestion, domains can be analysed in terms of spatial co-ordinates (overlapping points and features) and intensive ordinates (thresholds, gradients and levels). Based on this sketch two clinically salient points were made. Firstly, distress varies on a continuum ranging from a concentrated to a diffused ability to generate and inhabit domains. The circularity of body and world is such that distress becomes a kind of domain drift as the client moves into increasingly idiosyncratic milieus and slips away from shared or mutual ways of being. Secondly, formulating distress means returning to the events which characterise a domain. A map can be created which assists the client to understand and anticipate how a domain works. Exit points can then be considered; ways to extend the plane and initiate new ways of relating. Hope lies in creating interventions which help move the client along the embodied continuum. The therapist welcomes the client hoping that one day they might drift off.

References

Aho, J & Aho, K (2008). *Body Matters: A phenomenology of sickness, disease, and illness.* Plymouth: Lexington Books.

Artaud, A (1992). *Selected Writings.* Berkeley, CA: California University Press.

Beebe, B & Lachmann, M (2002). *Infant Research and Adult Treatment: Co-constructing interactions.* London: The Analytic Press.

Boston Change Process Group (1998). Non-interpretative mechanisms in psychoanalytic therapy: The something more than interpretation. *International Journal of Psychoanalysis*, *79*, 903–20.

Cash, T (2002). Cognitive-behavioral perspectives on body image. In T Cash & T Pruzinsky (Eds) *Body Image: A handbook of theory, research and clinical practice*. London: Guilford Press.

Cooper, M (2009). Welcoming the other: Actualising the humanistic ethic at the core of counselling psychology practice. *Counselling Psychology Review*, *24,* 119–30.

Damasio, A (2006). *Descartes' Error: Emotion, reason and the human body*. London: Vintage.

De Haan, S & Fuchs, T (2010). The ghost in the machine: Disembodiment in schizophrenia – two case studies. *Psychopathology*, *43*, 327–33.

De Jaegher, H & Di Paulo, E (2007). Participatory sense making: An enactive approach to social cognition. *Phenomenology and the Cognitive Sciences*, *6*, 485–507.

Deleuze, G (1968). *Difference and Repetition*. London: Athlone Press.

Deleuze, G (1970). *Spinoza: Practical philosophy*. San Francisco: City Lights.

Deleuze, G (1997). *Negotiations*. New York: Columbia University Press.

Deleuze, G (2006). *Dialogues II*. London: Continuum.

Deleuze, G & Guattari, F (1994). *What is Philosophy?* London: Verso.

Derrida, J (2000). *Of Hospitality*. Stanford, CA: Stanford University Press.

Deusund, L & Skarderud, F (2003). Use the body and forget the body: Treating anorexia nervosa with adapted physical activity. *Clinical Child Psychiatry and Psychology*, *8*, 53–72.

Diamond, N (2001). Towards an interpersonal understanding of bodily experience. *Psychodynamic Counselling, 7,* 41–62.

Foucault, M (1973). *The Birth of the Clinic: An archaeology of medical perception*. New York: Vintage.

Foucault, M (1989). *Madness and Civilisation: A history of insanity in the age of reason*. London: Routledge.

Freud, S & Breuer, J (2004). *Studies in Hysteria*. London: Penguin.

Fuchs, T (2005). Corporealised and disembodied minds: A phenomenological view of the body in melancholia and schizophrenia. *Philosophy, Psychiatry and Psychology*, *12*(2), 95–107.

Fuchs, T (2010). Embodiment, intersubjectivity and psychopathology. Paper presented to the Embodiment, intersubjectivity and psychopathology conference, Heidelberg (September).

Fuchs, T & De Jaegher, H (2010). Non-representational intersubjectivity. In T Fuchs, H Sattel & P Henningsen (Eds) *The Embodied Self: Dimensions, coherence and disorders*. Stuttgart: Schattauer.

Fuchs, T, Sattel, H & Henningsen, P (2010). *The Embodied Self: Dimensions, coherence and disorders*. Stuttgart: Schattauer.

Gallagher, S (2005). *How the Body Shapes the Mind*. Oxford: Oxford University Press.

Grant, A, Towned, M, Mills, J & Cockx, A (2008). *Assessment and Case Formulation in Cognitive Behavioural Therapy*. London: Sage.

Harvey, A, Watkins, E, Mansell, W & Shafran, R (2004). *Cognitive Behavioural Processes across Psychological Disorders: A transdiagnostic approach to research and treatment.* Oxford: Oxford University Press.

Hinshelwood, R (2001). *Thinking about Institutions: Milieux and madness.* London: Athenaeum Press.

Lakoff, G & Johnson, M (1999). *Philosophy in the Flesh: The embodied mind and its challenge to Western thought.* New York: Perseus Books.

Levinas, E (1999). *Otherwise than Being or Beyond Essence.* Pittsburgh, PA: Duquesne University Press.

Lewin, K (1936). *Principals of Topological Psychology.* New York: McGraw-Hill.

Krueger, D (1989). *Body Self and Psychological Self: A developmental and clinical integration of disorders of the self.* New York: Brunner.

McKay, M, Wood, J & Brantley, J (2007). *The Dialectical Behavior Skills Workbook: Practical DBT exercises for learning mindfulness, interpersonal effectiveness, emotion regulation and distress tolerance.* Oakland, CA: New Harbinger.

Merleau-Ponty, M (1962). *The Phenomenology of Perception.* London: Routledge.

Milner, P & Rose, N (1986). *The Power of Psychiatry.* Oxford: Polity.

Molbak, R (2007). A life of variable speeds: On constructing a Deleuzian psychotherapy. *Theory & Psychology, 17,* 473–90.

Ogden, P, Minton, K & Pain, C (2006). *Trauma and the Body: A sensorimotor approach to psychotherapy.* London: Norton.

Rumble, B (2009). A portfolio of academic, therapeutic practice and research work: Including an exploration of the client experience of the embodied client–therapist interaction. Unpublished doctoral dissertation, University of Surrey.

Rumble, B (2010). The body as hypothesis and as question: Towards a concept of therapist embodiment. *Body, Movement and Dance in Psychotherapy, 5,* 129–40.

Ryle, A & Kerr, I (2002). *Introducing Cognitive Analytic Therapy: Principals and practice.* Chichester: Wiley.

Sandler, J (1976). Countertransference and role-responsiveness. *International Review of Psychoanalysis, 3,* 43–7.

Segal, Z, Williams, J & Teasdale, J (2002). *Mindfulness-based Cognitive Therapy for Depression: A new approach to preventing relapse.* New York: Guilford Press.

Sheets-Johnstone, M (1999). *The Primacy of Movement.* Philadelphia, PA: John Benjamin Publishing.

Spurling, L (2004). *An Introduction to Psychodynamic Counselling.* Basingstoke: Palgrave Macmillan.

Stern, D (1985). *The Interpersonal World of the Infant: A view from psychoanalysis and developmental psychology.* London: Basic Books.

Stern, D (2010). *Forms of Vitality.* Oxford: Oxford University Press.

Strawbridge, S & Woolfe, R (2003). Counselling psychology in context. In R Woolfe, W Dryden & S Strawbridge (Eds) *Handbook of Counselling Psychology.* London: Sage.

Thelen, E & Smith, L (1996). *A Dynamic Systems Approach to the Development of Cognition and Action*. Cambridge, MA: MIT Press.

Thompson, E (2007). *Mind in Life: Biology, phenomenology and the sciences of the mind*. Cambridge, MA: Harvard University Press.

Trevarthen, C & Aitkin, K (2001). Infant intersubjectivity: Research, theory, and clinical applications. *Journal of Child Psychology and Psychiatry, 42*, 3–48.

Varela, F, Thompson, E & Rosch, E (1993). *The Embodied Mind: Cognitive science and human experience*. London: MIT Press.

Walsh, B (2005). *Treating Self-injury: A practical guide*. New York: Guilford Press.

Weiss, G (1999). *Body Images: Embodiment as intercorporeality*. New York: Routledge.

Woolfe, R, Dryden, W & Strawbridge, S (2003). *Handbook of Counselling Psychology*. London: Sage.

Epilogue: Going beyond diagnosis ...

Martin Milton

In the age of standardisation and the desire for complete and utter confidence in *knowing*, the one thing that I did not want for this book was a standardised approach to exploring 'psychopathology'. That has been done before – attempts exist in the form of the *DSM* and *ICD* and there are a myriad of other books that purport to define and instruct us in the treatment of 'disorders'. To have offered any kind of 'grand truth' about any diagnostic category or ways to 'treat' it would have been nothing but pointless duplication; far more importantly, it would have risked silencing even further the people we have worked with and learnt from. So I am delighted that the contributors took up the challenge to respond to the experiences they have had, rather than try to stick to any single game plan.

It seems to me that the variety of approaches and experiences that this book embodies is testament to the vagaries of life and the realities of therapeutic practice. While we may all have times when we want standardisation and clarity, we all know that people are unique, as are the contexts we inhabit and work in. There is no shortcut if we want fully to understand the meaning of a diagnosis; to enhance our understanding we have to approach the person with curiosity, we need to attempt a 'blank page' despite, sometimes quite extensive, referral letters or case notes. And this is what the contributors have offered us, insights into different experiences, the meanings that they can have for people and ways in which therapists can engage with people in our efforts to facilitate development or recovery.

Whether we think about 'common' experiences such as depression or the less frequently diagnosed problems of the personality disorders, it is evident that the distress people bring to therapy is painful and difficult. The contributors have reminded us though that these experiences are seldom meaningless. In fact, the chapters illuminate, in very different ways, the fact that as long as we go beyond our initial assumptions about a diagnostic category, we have the chance to engage with a range of people and the huge variety of meanings that inhabit these difficulties.

A key message to emanate from the preceding chapters is how important it is to begin by recognising the universality of human distress and our own potential to be, amongst other things, hurt, fearful, lost and confused. I would argue that this openness of spirit *has* to be there if we have any chance of truly approaching the therapeutic. So I applaud the courage of the contributors in engaging so personally and so fulsomely in this task and demonstrating *why* this personal engagement has to be present; why it is such an important part of the therapeutic process – whether or not it goes on to become an overt part of the therapeutic discussion. By engaging in this way we can capitalise on our shared humanity to help us understand the client, their distress and the therapeutic relationship.

So a key point raised by these chapters is that at best, diagnosis can only ever be a part of an experience. The contributors have given us their thoughts on how we may start to go beyond diagnosis and really engage with the more important tasks of understanding and supporting clients in their efforts to manage their distress. Understanding more fully, thinking more broadly and formulating in a more attuned fashion have all been put forward as ways in which we can move on. There is also the challenge of taking our thinking and knowledge out of the consulting room to intervene at a wider social and policy level too.

While our efforts in the consulting room may sometimes feel a bit modest, this is where we can at least start to get beyond the limits of diagnosis, where we realise that diagnoses are not inevitably meaningful, the label is not necessarily a truth. Counselling psychologists and other relational therapists recognise that individualised formulations open up vistas of meaning that are otherwise shut down. When prioritising a broad formulation, contributors (whether working from cognitive-behavioural, psychodynamic or other perspectives) have prompted us to think about the *meaning* of 'symptoms' and the ways in which symptoms and meanings can be held in mind together. Symptoms are meaningful signs that illuminate core emotional and relational concerns.

While manualised approaches may have their place as an initial guide, counselling psychologists and other relational therapists have long advocated the importance of developing individualised ways of working that come out of a personalised formulation. That way the therapy is more phenomenologically oriented at its very core, it evolves out of shared understandings in order to suit *this* client with their *specific* difficulties. This may require the therapist to take responsibility for a more pluralistic approach to practice so that as well as considering whether a therapist adopt either a CBT *or* a psychodynamic approach (as policy makers and insurance companies seem to assume is possible), counselling psychologists might also consider the contribution that psychodynamic thinking can offer their CBT work; or the systemic factors of their person-centred work and so forth. A thorough and disciplined study of different psychological and philosophical approaches to therapy helps therapists consider the meaning of an issue alongside the recommended 'technique'. An example of this is in Chapter 4 where Lucy Atcheson and I show how the power of the behavioural work traditionally advocated for people's phobic difficulties may be enhanced when the symptom becomes meaningful by having a relational and developmental account alongside the technique.

Of course, tailor-made thinking about symptoms and individually focused therapy soon brings home the fact that individualised work requires greater openness to broader understandings than are easily packaged. When we reflect critically on our clients' (and our own) struggles it is evident that it can be useful to bracket off the 'normal', taken-for-granted assumptions about people, health and illness. From there, it is only a short step to recognising that we might benefit from deconstructing the structures that lead to diagnosis and from re-thinking human emotional life more generally. In doing so we might recognise the links between the personal and the social, the micro and the macro. For example, we should not forget the power relations that bedevil us economically and socially and how these also affect our sense of self and our forms of relating. This wider, more relational form of critique also encourages us to recognise the problematic nature of binary views of gender as purely 'man' and (or versus) 'woman' so that we might hear about the various other experiences of gender that, in reality, populate the wide spectrum of gendered experiences. The same with sexuality, as distress emanates from the false understanding of people as *either* heterosexual (sometimes viewed as 'normal') *or* gay (often read as 'problematic'). To fully understand the place of sexuality in people's lives we need to recognise the multiplicity of positions that can be adopted in a fluid manner throughout the lifespan. More critical thinking might also give us the chance to reflect on the damage caused by the limitations of the class systems we inhabit, the generational effects of colonialism, genocide and slavery and of other forms of historical trauma.

Such a deconstructive stance is a bit like any other therapeutic ingredient – not always possible in a therapy situation, nor inevitably appropriate. Having said that I suspect the *thinking* is always appropriate but whether we translate that into actual dialogue is a more individualised and sophisticated decision to be made in the context of a specific therapy. This isn't always the key agenda for individual therapy as it may not be meaningful to the client, it may not be possible in our time-limited approaches and sometimes such 'deviations from protocol' are formally discouraged by guidelines and treatment manuals as these documents seem to consider the social and political domain as separate to the psychological, and the fact that knowledge about populations is separate to individuals' meaning-making.

Whatever challenges occur, the importance of engaging critically at all levels remains an ethical responsibility for us all. As Roly Fletcher and Lucy Atcheson touch on, counselling psychologists (as professionals and as citizens) may well have roles outside of the consulting room and we can be open to the ways in which we inform service structures and public discussions about different psychological difficulties and their development. This might at least allow us to limit some of the damaging stigma that underpins much psychological difficulty. As contributors point out, all the time people laugh at phobias, ignore the depressed, abuse the traumatised we victimise even more people.

Whatever our hopes and aims for this book, the contributors and I know that it is only one step in an ongoing discussion. We hope that readers have found something to agree with, something to be surprised about and some things that they would want to challenge. In doing so we hope that readers take us up on the invitation to go beyond diagnosis in their professional activities and in their personal lives.

Contributors

Editor

Dr Martin Milton is a chartered psychologist and registered psychotherapist working in independent practice and in the School of Psychology at the University of Surrey. He is editor of *Therapy and Beyond: Counselling psychology contributions to therapeutic and social issues* and has published in a range of academic journals. Martin is on the editorial board of *Ecopsychology*, *Counselling Psychology Review* and *Psychology of Sexualities Review*.

Contributors

Dr Lucy Atcheson is a chartered psychologist and registered counselling psychologist and trained at the University of Surrey. She has worked in the public and private sector with a range of client groups. She has also disseminated psychological knowledge through her work on television and through her recent books.

Dr Terry Boucher is a registered psychologist working in a specialist pain management service within the NHS. He trained at the University of Surrey and has a special interest in relational aspects of the therapeutic setting.

Dr Louise Brorstrom is a counselling psychologist who works for the NHS in a community mental health team. She trained at the University of Surrey and has strong clinical and research interests in traumatic experiences and the socio-political impact of trauma therapy.

Dr Roly Fletcher is a chartered psychologist working in a secondary care NHS setting and trained at the University of Surrey.

Dr Joanna Jackson is a registered counselling psychologist who has worked within the NHS across a range of primary, secondary and tertiary services since 2004. She trained at the University of Surrey and was recently awarded the prize for 'Excellence in Research' by the BPS Division of Counselling Psychology.

Dr Tim Knowlson is a registered counselling psychologist with the Health Professions Council and a chartered psychologist with the British Psychological Society. Tim completed his PsychD in psychotherapeutic and counselling psychology at the University of Surrey and has worked in the NHS in a variety of settings including primary care, community mental health teams and psychotherapy services.

Dr Ben Rumble is a specialist counselling psychologist with the Sussex Partnership NHS Foundation Trust working in acute care. He trained at the University of Surrey where his research focused on embodiment and psychotherapy. The chapter on domains reflects his interest in models of distress which draw on enactive cognitive science and the work of Deleuze and Guattari.

Index

working alliance (*see also* therapeutic
        relationship) 41
World Health Organization (WHO) xii,
        xvi, 2, 10, 15, 16, 32, 65, 76, 79, 92

Y
Yalom, I 5, 10, 21, 32

Psychology in the Real World: Community-based groupwork
Guy Holmes
ISBN 978 1 906254 13 1   £21.99

Guy Holmes describes projects recognised nationally for their innovation and importance, as a response to repeated requests to the author to help set up similar projects. This book, in everyday language, bridges the gap between community psychology and group theory and practice. It is a 'how to' guide, giving practical suggestions on new ways to provide psychological services, combat stigma, help people to escape toxic mental environments, think about medication and bring about meaningful service-user involvement.

Person-Centered and Experential Therapies Work: A review of the research on counseling, psychotherapy and related practices
Mick Cooper, Jeanne C. Watson & Dagmar Hölldampf (eds)
ISBN 978 1 906254 25 4   £22.00

Government attempts to streamline and standardise psychotherapy services – favouring Cognitive-Behaviour Therapy – mean that many PCE practitioners are under pressure to justify their work. At the same time, research is now an essential component of the counselling and psychotherapy curriculum at undergraduate as well as postgraduate level. Hence both students and practitioners will welcome this important volume, which brings together the existing and impressive evidence base for PCE therapies, as well as providing pointers to areas where research is lacking.

Qualitative Research in Arts and Mental Health: Contexts, meanings and evidence
Theo Stickley (ed)
ISBN 978 1 906254 39 1   £22.00

This is the first book published in the UK that brings together key research studies providing evidence to support the use of participatory arts in improving mental health. It is a timely publication in the context of tremendous growth in policy support and practice development of Arts and Health. Each chapter describes a research study underpinned by rigorous evaluation and sound research methodology, exploring the meanings and processes that frame creative participation, examining issues of stigma, recovery, inclusion, connectivity and belonging through art in a wide a range of settings.

PCCS Books   www.pccs-books.co.uk   +44(0)1989 763900